Holy Divorce

A Mindful and Spiritual Act of Self-love

BARBARA KIAO, L.C.C.

BALBOA.
PRESS
A DIVISION OF HAY HOUSE

Balboa Press books may be ordered through booksellers or by contacting:

Balboa Press
A Division of Hay House
1663 Liberty Drive
Bloomington, IN 47403
www.balboapress.com.au
1 (877) 407-4847

Because of the dynamic nature of the Internet, any web addresses or
links contained in this book may have changed since publication and
may no longer be valid. The views expressed in this work are solely those
of the author and do not necessarily reflect the views of the publisher,
and the publisher hereby disclaims any responsibility for them.

The author of this book does not dispense medical advice or prescribe the use
of any technique as a form of treatment for physical, emotional, or medical
problems without the advice of a physician, either directly or indirectly. The
intent of the author is only to offer information of a general nature to help you
in your quest for emotional and spiritual well-being. In the event you use any
of the information in this book for yourself, which is your constitutional right,
the author and the publisher assume no responsibility for your actions.

Any people depicted in stock imagery provided by Thinkstock are models,
and such images are being used for illustrative purposes only.
Certain stock imagery © Thinkstock.

Printed in the United States of America.

ISBN: 978-1-4525-2413-9 (sc)
ISBN: 978-1-4525-2414-6 (e)

Balboa Press rev. date: 09/23/2014

CONTENTS

Acknowledgments

This is my virgin book, and even I know that it takes more than one person to have it published.

I would like to thank the team at Balboa for their patience and kind assistance.

To my past and present clients, you inspire me and keep me grounded.

There are others (mainly close friends) who have encouraged and supported me. There are also those who doubted the idea of a published book. You too have given me the will to complete this book.

Last but not least, to my beloved parents and sister, for giving me the strength and inspiration to lead an authentic life, my undying love always. I am who I am because you loved me the way you best knew how.

INTRODUCTION

In the beginning, I wanted to shout from the rooftops that I had been wronged (wronged, you hear?) by my deceiving husband of twenty-four years. I was full of anger, if not rage, and I didn't know it. But writing helped me process my hurt emotions (both conscious and subconscious). I slowly found myself embarking on a spiritual journey that not only was healing but also allowed me to establish a connection to my authentic self.

I no longer want the world's sympathy, nor do I wish to make myself the victim of my life's lessons. I no longer yearn for justice—and definitely not vengeance. What I do want is to share my experience with you, the readers, so that women and men, young and old alike, can learn from the mistakes I made. I want to share this empowering knowledge that can bring you face-to-face with your own shadows, your dark side. I want you to join me in the journey to the place where you can begin to learn, to accept, to embrace, and ultimately to love that part of you that you so desperately wish to hide and shun.

Drawing on both my professional and personal experience, I share with you healthy ways to face your own fears, which will enable you to reach your highest self-understanding and fulfillment of your authentic self—and create true love and happiness.

As Robin Holden said, "Our purpose in life is to learn to love and be loved."

ACT 1

Reality Hits

When someone shows you who they
are, believe them the first time!

Maya Angelou

Scene 1

EMOTIONAL TSUNAMI

Shanghai, PR China

Bad Boy: "Hi, baby, I am back; tight hug and soft kisses."

Cowgirl: "With warm and wet lips ... sweet kisses."

Bad Boy: "Hmm, sounds very good to me ..."

Cowgirl: "U r tired from paddling?"

Bad Boy: "No, not really. Didn't go on the boat, had to prepare for filming by two different TV stations."

Cowgirl: "Okay, was thinking, I'd love to give ya a nice massage on ur head and back."

Bad Boy: "YEEEEEESSSSS?????"

Cowgirl: "When u lie between my legs, I can give nice head massage."

Bad Boy: "I want it all over ..."

Cowgirl: "I am a bad, bad, bad girl!"

Bad Boy: "Never mind my head … oh, maybe the other one!"

Cowgirl: "Back scratch should be comfy."

Bad Boy: "We know how bad you are—not badder than me, though!"

Cowgirl: "Ha-ha!"

Bad Boy: "I am the real bad, bad one … dirty mind, horny all the time …"

Cowgirl: "Thinking of you makes me horny now …"

Bad Boy: "You are getting to me too, playing the same movie in my head, over and over …"

Cowgirl: "I don't really want to become a juicy fruit right here in the office …"

Bad Boy: "That's okay, but you'll notice that you are becoming wet."

Cowgirl: "What if I want to come?"

Bad Boy: "Go to the little girl's room, and just help yourself. You're also making me hard … thank God I've got a desk to hide it."

Cowgirl: "Ha-ha, this is totally bad, bad, bad!"

Bad Boy: "I think tomorrow we'll both have a problem! When you arrive, I need to do a room inspection FIRST THING, to make sure you are satisfied with the service, facilities, and all, but I also have to be on time for dinner, so people don't get suspicious."

Cowgirl: "Well, I'm not sure. How would that work?"

Bad Boy: "Wear something easy to remove and put back on."

Cowgirl: "Ha-ha, this is just bad, bad, bad, man! It's summertime, anyway, things are easy to remove ... I'm soaking wet now, baby!"

Bad Boy: "Want me come over?"

Cowgirl: "Yup."

Bad Boy: "I love a wet girl ..."

Cowgirl: "Nah, I am a juicy fruit!"

Bad Boy: "Like to taste that juicy, sweet fruit ... would u like that?"

Cowgirl: "Wet?"

Bad Boy: "Me tasting it."

Cowgirl: "Sure, I would love that."

Bad Boy: "Good! Did I tell you before that I cannot make babies anymore? Got 'clipped' after my second daughter was born."

Cowgirl: "So?"

Bad Boy: "So I only shoot blank ammunition."

Cowgirl: "I don't mind! Ha-ha, we are talking like we are going to do something bad right now."

Bad Boy: "That's right, exactly. I am sooo ready! But it's not bad; it's something wonderful to enjoy. We need to do it slowly and take our time."

Cowgirl: "I have time, plenty of time; but we don't have a venue."

Bad Boy: "I love to touch, kiss, and cuddle as long as possible. We can meet in your room. Remember, you need to do an in-depth interview with this BAD BOY! I'll call you when I can come to your room, and you just keep the door open. Is your number still 555-348?"

Cowgirl: "Aren't there monitors in the hotel? You're not afraid people will see u on the video? I don't feel safe."

Bad Boy: "Of course there are, but I'm wearing my hat, sunglasses, bandana, and a pipe."

Cowgirl: "Ha-ha. Oh God, u r cute, man!"

Bad Boy: "Don't worry, I run this place. Nobody will disturb us."

Cowgirl: "But I feel—"

Bad Boy: "You are sitting at my table tomorrow. Can't wait to be close to you."

Cowgirl: "You have the seating arrangement? Am I right next to you, darling? Now I'm nervous, when it's really coming to reality …"

Bad Boy: "I told May that you are the only one I know and the only one who speaks English, so yeah, probably."

Cowgirl: "What shall I wear to impress you?"

Bad Boy: "You impress me wearing absolutely NOTHING, but not there. My little secretary will probably sit next to me too."

Cowgirl: "Little? I'm not sure I met her."

Bad Boy: "She's short, on the plump side, and just out of college. Not my taste, though, if u know what I mean. I like strong, intelligent, cuddly, and sexy women."

Cowgirl: "U r telling me I'm your type?"

Bad Boy: "Wouldn't do this if you weren't my type. I am VERY selective and haven't had a lover in years. Just fell for you when we met last year, I guess, but didn't want to push it. Wasn't sure if you wanted it."

Cowgirl: "Well, I had a crush on u and didn't dare even mention it, and u asked if u could drop by when visiting Shanghai and have a drink, but we never did."

Bad Boy: "True—I was never alone."

Cowgirl: "So can I be your little secret lover?"

Bad Boy: "Sure can … I like that!"

Cowgirl: "What does a lover need to do?"

Bad Boy: "I don't want you to do something you feel awkward about … you always need two to tango!"

Cowgirl: "We'll do whatever I feel like doing: think about u, dream about u, talk to u in my mind, picture your strong arms holding me tight."

Bad Boy: "And I'll always honor your wishes."

Cowgirl: "I do think u r strong enough to be my man!"

Bad Boy: "Are you strong enough to be 'just a little lover'?"

Cowgirl: "I am definitely strong enough to be your woman!"

Bad Boy: "Women ALWAYS have to pull the short end of the stick, and you know my situation here. But yes, I'd like u to be my woman. Gotta run, will talk again when the coast is clear."

Treasure could not bring herself to continue reading the rest of the saved messages. She sat in front of Xavier's computer, feeling numb yet abnormally calm. She wanted to cry, but in her shell-shocked state, there were no tears, just horror. *This cannot be happening to me. Not my Xavier, not me!*

As her mind whirled, she suddenly realized she knew the identity of "Cowgirl." Almost immediately another woman's image popped into her head: Heather. If Xavier could have had a thing with Cowgirl, surely he would also take advantage of Heather.

Heather was the girlfriend of one of Xavier's corporate clients. She was well-known to be desperately seeking men. Treasure even teased Xavier that she had a crush on him. Little did she know Xavier had already used Heather for his own selfish needs.

Before her mind could even make a decision, her fingers had moved ahead, doing the thinking for her.

Another file was open, and Treasure's suspicions were confirmed; a photo of Heather, topless, stared back at her from the computer screen.

By now Treasure had stopped thinking altogether. She was on autopilot, focused on finding out everything she could. She could no longer hide from the ugly truth; she had to face it. Heart pounding, she double-clicked the files "ME2001," "ME2002," and "ME2003"—pictures of Xavier posing nude in front of a camera. These pictures were definitely not intended for his wife. Tears started to roll from her hazel eyes, but she ignored them. Her index finger on the mouse went faster and faster, closing and opening different files. There were photos of women she recognized and some she did not. She found Xavier in chat rooms and on porn sites, looking for women to be "friends … discreetly."

At least he did say he's married and needs to be discreet, Treasure thought, trying to be positive. But then she came across a hermaphrodite, looking at the woman with both breasts and a penis. She could no longer restrain her professional mind; Xavier needed professional intervention. Treasure's head was spinning with a million questions.

How could I have missed this? Why didn't I see that he's a cheat? Why was I so blind? What should I do now? Do I still love him? Does he still love me? Could I ever trust him again? What's going to happen to us? Was he abused when he was young? Was he molested as a child? Maybe he's a closet gay or bisexual? What's going to happen to Sabrina and Vanessa when they find out their father has done it again? Old wounds will definitely reopen, damn him. Damn Xavier!

Scene 2

OUR FIRST SESSION

Brisbane, Australia

It was a cool autumn day when I first laid eyes on Treasure. She was sitting in the waiting room, busily completing forms.

When she walked into my office, Treasure greeted me with a broad smile and firm handshake. She had a sincere smile, and since I like a firm handshake, I couldn't help but take an instant liking to her.

My first impression of Treasure was that she was an attractive woman, extremely well dressed, with excellent taste. She was stylish, sophisticated, intelligent, and a possible perfectionist. In short, she looked like a woman who had it all. I was curious to learn the reasons that had brought her to my office.

"Hi, Dr. Adams, how would you like me to address you—Dr. Adams or Alicia?" she began.

"Please call me Alicia," I replied. "I'm not big on formality. Please, make yourself comfortable."

"Thank you, Alicia. Where do I begin? I am Australian, but my husband and I are now living in Shanghai, China. We have been married for twenty-four years. About a month ago, I found out he's been cheating on me for a decade. Needless to say, I was devastated and absolutely shocked. Now I'm just angry, and I still can't quite believe it."

I have been counseling for more than twenty years, and it takes a lot to shock me. But I was stunned by the similarity of our predicaments. I tried to keep my facial expression in check, hoping Treasure wouldn't pick up on my uneasiness. "I see. Please tell me more," I replied.

"As it turns out, I knew all the women that he slept with—well, as far as I know, anyway! I'm sure he had others, but I don't want to think about that. The first betrayal happened while we were living in Kota Kinabalu, East Malaysia, and he was pre-opening a hotel. Her name was Mickey, and I used to counsel her—I can't believe it! She even sent me birthday and Christmas cards each year, thanking me for the help that I gave her … blah blah blah. Gosh, it makes me sick! I don't know how she could face herself. You know, I told Xavier to write to all those women and to apologize for using them as sex objects. He's been in touch with all of them. It's just sick! Sorry, Alicia, I'm not talking sense, am I?"

"You're talking fast; slow down. How did you find out?"

"Oh, I guess I was ready to find out, and I believe that subconsciously he wanted to be found out. One weekend I was relaxing in front of the TV, and Xavier yelled out to me from the study: 'Hey, did I tell you Chelsea's married?' He wanted me to look at her wedding photos. Actually, I got a bit annoyed—he kept on asking me to look at her wedding photos, and I don't know the woman well and really had no interest in her wedding photos. When he wouldn't stop pestering me, I gave in. He was still looking at the computer screen as I approached him, when suddenly he looked anxious and quickly exclaimed he had deleted the file by mistake. I found his behavior strange but decided I would try to be helpful and locate the file for him the next morning—after all; Xavier is a bit technically challenged. I've asked to use his computer before so I decided to just go ahead with it. You know the funny part? He, who has everything to hide, doesn't even have a password, and yet I, who have nothing to hide, do!"

"What did you find?" I asked.

"Well, my intention was just to find Chelsea's wedding photos, and when I did, it slowly dawned on me that Xavier could be hiding something. Call it a hunch. I decided to check other files, and that's when I saw the MSN messages between the two. He called himself Bad Boy and her Cowgirl. I have no words to describe how I felt, except that I was suffocating in a tsunami of mixed emotions that I didn't even know I had—I immediately thought that this must be what death feels like."

"Do you have suicidal thoughts?" I asked.

"Oh no, are you kidding me? He's not worth it! Sorry, I didn't mean my own death—I just meant death in general, though my Mom did kill herself. I guess I'm relating this trauma to the trauma of my Mom's death."

"I am so sorry, Treasure. How old were you when your mom committed suicide?"

"Well, I was twenty-five, but honestly, I don't think my age at the time matters; I would have been devastated no matter what age I'd been, because I considered her my protector. It might have been easier on me if she had died of natural causes, but she took her own life. I think unconsciously I felt she'd abandoned me, and therefore I was attracted to Xavier. You don't need me to tell you how it works with our human psyche; what we didn't understand, we will reenact in order to heal and process those emotions. Do you agree with my analysis, Dr. Adams … Alicia?"

"Yes, Treasure, it's highly possible," I replied with a smile, beginning to notice that Treasure was doing my job as well.

"Soon after I confronted him, I ran, sobbing nonstop, and hid in the walk-in closet. He tried to hold me, but I pushed him away and screamed to him that he had 'committed suicide' with our marriage. Alicia, I do not believe in coincidences, and I believe everything happens for a reason. You have no idea—I so wanted someone to hold me that very moment. I felt so alone and helpless. But how could I let the same person who hurt me comfort me, right? Not only that, I also called him an asshole, and I said if he's an asshole, and I'm married to him, what would that make me? Mrs. Asshole, right? And I told him I didn't want to be Mrs. Asshole, so I had no choice but to leave him. As soon as I spat that out, I knew that he had finally broken the camel's back—I no longer wished to be his wife. It was then. But I'm not so sure what to think now."

"Yes, Treasure, it's absolutely understandable how you felt, and it takes courage to get professional help," I agreed, secretly thinking that she was a much stronger woman than I am. All of a sudden, I felt like a fraud being her therapist.

"Well, I did not manage to find him out all these years. There's something there, right? I need to find out the role I played in all of this, or I'll attract the same type of man again. With 20/20 hindsight, I always knew something was not quite right, but I could never put my finger on it. He was never 100 percent present; he was neither here nor there. I suppose it's easier to be in denial and not examine what you know needs to be looked at. But he got worse as he aged. It was when we were still living in Nanjing, China that it got worse."

Scene 3

DUTIFUL WIFE:
HER "LOVING TOO MUCH"

Brisbane, Australia

"Hi, Treasure, come on in. How have you been since last week?" I asked.

"I'm fine—all things considered," came her reply. "I can't believe this is going to be our last session before I go back to Shanghai to face the music. I am so dreading it."

"That's completely understandable," I reassured her, adding, "I was quite surprised that you came back for more sessions."

"Oh? Why would you think that?" Treasure gave me a puzzled look.

"Because I always knew you would know what's right for you, with or without me working with you," I responded.

"Thank you, Alicia, but you know, I find myself less anxious after our sessions, because I don't have to explain myself to you like I do with laypeople. I'm coming back in October," she said and smiled, "so you're not getting rid of me yet."

Somehow, I felt flattered. "Well, thank you, Treasure. I enjoy talking with you too." I couldn't help but wonder what she'd think of me if she knew how much I had looked forward to our weekly sessions for the past few months. Deep down I so wanted to find out whether she would leave or stay with Xavier. The personal side of me so wanted to see if I could learn from Treasure's experience.

After a short silence, Treasure continued. "You know, I've been wondering why I married someone whom I don't consider my best friend. Okay, sure, I thought he was a good catch when we first met. I find him charming, sexy, and dynamic. Many people commented that we looked perfect together, and we played the part of a handsome couple. He's always doing little things for me; he sent me love notes and flowers on Valentine's Day. We often went dancing because I love to dance, and he even learned to play tennis because it's my passion. But the tennis and dancing all stopped soon after we got married. Last year for my birthday, he gave me a surprise first-class ticket to Chicago to see *The Oprah Winfrey Show*. He knows Oprah is my idol and that I longed to see her in person. I was so touched by his thoughtfulness and the effort he had put into making it happen. I felt loved, and I'm sure all people thought I was. I was the envy of all my friends and Liz, my sister. For crying out loud, I was the envy of myself, and it came as a shock to all my friends when I found him out, most of all me!

"I keep thinking back to how we couldn't keep our hands off each other in the beginning, always hugging and holding hands. I guess the only thing that really bothered me about him was his insensitivity. Of course, now I know it's more than that."

There was sadness in Treasure's voice as she continued. "He used to tell everyone I was his best friend, and I'd bluntly announce that he wasn't mine. He never expressed how he felt by my comment, and I guess I spoke out of resentment toward his lack of emotional support of me all those years. I was so ready to move back to Australia the year he got another transfer from J. B. to K. K."

"Where exactly is that?" I asked.

"Oh, sorry. J. B. is Johor Bahru, the Malaysian city that's a causeway away from Singapore, and K. K. is Kota Kinnabalu, on the island of Borneo, in East Malaysia. Have you heard of Mount Kota Kinnabalu, Mount K. K. in short?"

"I do now, and I did remember you mentioning Xavier was pre-opening a hotel in Kota Kinnabalu at our first meeting."

"Yes, you have a good memory. He wanted my bonus children and me to climb Mount K. K. with him on his fiftieth birthday."

"Did you?" I asked.

"Yes, of course. It was his birthday wish," Treasure said simply. "I can't say the same for the children. They complained to me about Xavier's selfishness and how he always would insist on doing the things only he enjoys doing, with no thoughts for what anyone else wanted to do. Funny enough, I really had no idea what they were referring to at the time. Sure, I knew he could be selfish at times, but forcing people to do things only he likes? But now I see that I was oblivious to his behavior, because I was so focused on pleasing him, thinking that by doing so, he would appreciate the love, accommodation, and sacrifices, and that he'd reciprocate."

"Would you like to elaborate on that?" I urged Treasure to continue with her thoughts.

"You know the song lyric 'I can see clearly now the rain's gone, I can see all obstacles in my way'? Now that I'm out of my own way, I can see that I'm my own worst enemy. I so desperately wanted to see what I wanted to see in him." Treasure let out a long sigh.

I did know the song Treasure was referring to, but I decided to move my questioning in a different direction. "What do you mean by bonus children?"

"Ah, that. Xavier has two lovely daughters: Sabrina, the elder, and Vanessa, both from a previous marriage. I love them dearly. All the credit for raising them so well goes to his ex-wife, Michellene. I've always liked his ex-wife. For obvious reasons, the feeling wasn't mutual when we first met. Vanessa told me a long time ago that Michellene thought I was the other woman, and that she was like a single parent, because Xavier was never home to give her the support she needed or be a present father. She was really miserable at the time, but she's also a strong lady; she left Xavier after eleven years of marriage. Anyway, I don't like the terms *stepmother* and *stepchildren*, so I call them my bonus children, and myself their bonus mother."

"I like that; it's quite special." I was impressed by Treasure's creative thinking.

"Yes, I thought so. They're special to me. It saddens me that if I choose to leave Xavier, it will reopen old wounds for Sabrina and Vanessa. After all, it'll bring back painful childhood memories of when he was an absent father and that he also cheated on their mother, which led to their divorce. History is repeating itself. I remember my best friend in J. B. at the time told me she knew I wasn't happy continuing living in Malaysia and that I should tell Xavier."

"Did you?"

"No, I didn't. I told her that there would be no point, because I knew he wouldn't move back to Australia for me. He had been assigned to pre-open another hotel in K. K., and in the hospitality industry that is regarded as a prestigious promotion. I guess what I really wanted to say is that if I had him choose between me and his job, he would definitely choose the latter, and what would I do then?"

"I see. So, you assumed that he would ignore your feelings, and in fear of being rejected, you decided to sacrifice your happiness for him? Is that how it works in your relationship?" I asked.

"Wow, I didn't think of it that way. Hearing you say it, I guess I did, didn't I? I suppose I always knew he puts his interests before mine. I just wasn't ready to admit to it; otherwise, I would have to choose whether to stay with him or to leave him. I guess I've postponed the decision till now," Treasure said with a sad grin.

I was glad Treasure agreed with my assessment without any resistance. It showed she was ready to deal with her true emotions and reality.

"Alicia, by then we'd already been married for eleven years. Hey, it seems his cycle is eleven years instead of the usual seven-year itch. When I look back now, I believe the reason that I was so unhappy and wanted to move back to Australia was this: ever since we've been married, I always felt something was not quite right, I told you this

22

before. But I can't quite put my finger on it. I remember one time we had a big argument over my feeling upset with one of our friends. I expected him to stand by me, or at least to acknowledge my feelings, but instead he devalued my feelings by saying, 'I simply don't understand why you feel so upset. What's the big deal?' As a matter of fact, this was his favorite line; he never understands and he's never there to give me emotional support. In recent years, I feel like I'm losing myself. His 'I love you,' which he says to me daily, doesn't necessarily indicate what is going on in our relationship. I know that it is behavior, and not words, that defines reality. Alicia, I guess I was just too scared to challenge it head-on. Now I learn you can run, but you cannot hide, and my fear has finally caught up with me. You know what? The saddest thing is that I didn't confront Xavier with how I truly felt. If I had, I would have found out the truth—he does not care about my feelings or needs. The irony is that it all started in K. K. I remember he would pick fights with me regularly. Obviously, it was his tactic to allow himself to feel less guilty going to that woman. I really should have confronted him then."

Treasure looked out of the window, and although I couldn't see her face, I knew tears had welled up in her eyes again. After a few seconds, she turned and continued. "That year in K. K., I celebrated my fortieth, and we had invited close friends from all over the world to celebrate. I thought he was expressing his love when he arranged all the activities and accommodations for our guests. Mind you, he only complied with my request; nevertheless, I appreciated what appeared to be loving gestures. In reality, all along he felt the pressure of the pre-opening project and probably took the organizing of the birthday party as another task on the 'to-do list' but was unable to share his feelings with me. We had a black-tie event on the Saturday, followed by a sunset cruise the following day. The celebration was to last for three days. The Saturday evening of the black-tie event, everyone was having fun, enjoying the good food and wine, and dancing to lovely music. I was having such bliss that I was not paying attention to him. He didn't even ask me to dance, so, I just presumed he was also having fun with our friends. At around 11:30 that night, Xavier approached my table and, with a stern look on his face, announced to everyone that it was late and they should all go home (meaning back to their hotel rooms)."

"Really? How did you react?" I asked with disbelief.

"I was shocked at first, but I remember anger set in pretty fast."

"What about your guests?"

"Shocked as well; all eyes were on me. I felt so embarrassed and humiliated."

"What did you do?" I asked.

"I don't remember exactly, but the party mood was definitely killed instantly. It was a normal celebration the next day, but I knew my guests were all wondering what was with Xavier the night before. Nobody mentioned anything until weeks later. I remember we had our worst quarrel soon after the last guest departed. I confronted him, and he insisted he did nothing wrong. His reasoning was that he was only concerned for our guests. Up till today he has not apologized—just like other times that he behaved insensitively and unlovingly, I kept on giving him excuses and letting it slide. Even my friends defended his disrespectful behavior, due to his immense pressure with the hotel project. Now I see what we were all doing: we were *rationalizing*. Boy, did I rationalize my way out of any insights that interfered with my good feelings. I kept on telling myself, *I love him, and he's a good man. I've made him a promise that I'll stay with him till death do us part.* It only makes sense; it's my way of making the unacceptable acceptable! I was loving him too much! I failed to set boundaries with him. I simply enabled him to disrespect me. Hey, I just had a *bing-bing* moment."

"What do you mean?" I asked with great anticipation.

"By allowing him to disrespect me, I was disrespecting myself. Wow, I just realized that now," Treasure replied with eyes wide open.

Treasure stopped, and as I was about to question her, she continued. "When we first got married, we were both in managerial positions, working in the same hotel, and I remember one time I had issues with the hotel owners where things got so bad that I lost a lot of weight and had no appetite. Even then he showed no interest in what was happening. He clearly knew I was depressed, but not once did he ask me what was happening or try to comfort me."

Treasure began to cry as she recalled several other humiliating incidents in which Xavier appeared uninterested, cold, and insensitive to her needs. When confronted he would always use the excuse of not wanting to fight because that's the reason he divorced Michellene.

"Not for a million years did I think this could happen to me, to us. I never dreamed that the person I so totally trusted would betray me. It's like a dagger put straight into my heart. I loved and supported him for twenty-four years, through thick and thin. When he lost his job a couple of times, I stood by him and gave him encouragement. We have a long history together; and we definitely shared some wonderful years. I always thought he treasured what we had built together, the same way I did. I had counted on him to love and protect our life and me. Alicia, you told me you always knew I'd know what to do. At this moment, I can say you're dead wrong. I'm trying desperately to gain control of my life. It's a fucking mess. I fucking hate him. I'm not sure if I'll ever recover from this ... ever!"

Treasure's anger soon turned into tears; and tears turned into an uncontrollable sobbing of pain and despair.

Yes, *betrayal;* a dark, torturous, jagged edge to the word. Not only did I know her sense of devastation, but I could also feel her defeat, her loneliness, her pain, her fear, and the damage that went with it all.

I assured Treasure we would take a hard look at her relationship with Xavier and that when she had her answers, she would feel less overwhelmed. Together, we would find her true self again.

When she left my office that day, I began to feel shaky. Treasure's story hit me hard, *real* hard. I knew as her counselor that my reactions are important tools. It was important I make emotional connections with Treasure, to help me understand more quickly how she was feeling. But this was something more and much bigger. I couldn't help but feel extremely uneasy. This was not the first time a woman client had come to see me with this type of issue, nor was it the first time I reacted strongly. What I could no longer deny was that Treasure's situation was too close to my own.

On the outside, I appeared confident, fulfilled—a woman who truly had it all. In my practice I worked hard with clients to help them find confidence and a renewed sense of their authentic self and self-esteem. But at home it was another story. My husband, like Treasure's, was charming and romantic, and I had fallen madly in love with him almost immediately after we met. But I soon discovered that he had a great deal of anger, insecurities, and resentment inside him. He pushed my buttons in so many ways that I think he enjoyed seeing me feeling inadequate and off-balance.

The Alicia who was a therapist could say to Treasure, "Your husband's behavior doesn't sound loving. In fact, it sounds as if there's a lot of psychological abuse going on." But what was I saying to myself? The Alicia who went home at night twisted herself into a pretzel trying to keep her husband from stonewalling or picking fights with her. That Alicia kept telling herself that he was a wonderful man, that he was exciting to be with, and that if something went wrong, then it must be her fault.

I am not exempted from the disease of loving the man in my life too much by having no boundaries and somehow losing myself along the way! I also had disrespected myself by allowing him to disrespect me … my feelings, my needs.

The following week, Treasure sat herself down gently on my sofa and said, "Soon after I found out about Xavier's philandering, I demanded he apologizes to Michellene, Sabrina, and Vanessa, and even to write to all those women he had sex with, apologizing to them for exploiting them. Most are half his age, and as you know, I'm pretty sure he's using sex with them to regulate his negative emotions and his own inadequacies, and to boost his own ego. Probably that's also the reason I'm not that angry with the women, because I know they are in the same boat. The only person I didn't ask him to apologize to is the prostitute he loaned money to. I now see that that was my way of imposing a false sense of control. I'm sure it wouldn't be the first time I've done this, at least not consciously—tried to impose control—and this may be why he perceives me as having the power to frustrate him, to withhold love from him, to make him feel weak, or to make endless demands on him, all of which could trigger his childhood insecurities and hurt. That is why he always accuses me of trying to change him."

"Treasure, I believe you're on to something here. Are you telling me he visits prostitutes regularly?" I was surprised by the new information.

"I'm not sure. I only know of one," Treasure replied casually.

"How did you come to know about her?"

"Well, I saw her photo with him in his computer. I didn't know at first she was a prostitute, but I saw he wrote in his little black book a female's name, and that she owed him 2,500 RMB (about $400). I confronted him and he told me she's a hooker and that he felt sorry for her poor background and therefore loaned her the money. I can't believe he's so stupid to believe she's going to return his money. Of course, she has never been found since. You know he also introduced the women to me? It's so humiliating and disrespectful. If I had a gun I would have shot him right there and then!"

My alarm must have shown in my expression. Treasure quickly added, "Don't worry; he's not worth going to jail for! But I will admit to a *Godfather* fantasy—having the power to have Xavier 'disappeared' from this earth, and for him to know that it was me who ordered his death. That's the devil in me," Treasure exclaimed with a wicked smile.

She was still engrossed in her fantasy when I said, "Treasure, what you're feeling is absolutely normal. Your identity has been assaulted and your anger toward Xavier is justifiable. All your hurt feelings are still very raw, and you're in a great deal of pain. You are absolutely traumatized. But my immediate concern for you is whether Xavier's encounter with the prostitute and all the other women exposed you to STD."

"Thanks, Alicia, for your concern. I was also worried when I first found out. Although we had not made love for quite some time, one can never be too careful. I also ordered him to check for STDs, and his physician gave him a clean bill of health. You have no idea how relieved I was when I also got a negative result."

"Great. I'm glad to hear that."

"You know what his therapist told me about his introducing those women to me? She suspected that it was Xavier's way of saying 'up yours' twice. Do you think this is an accurate interpretation?"

I was dumbfounded by the therapist's unfounded judgment, and I asked, "Do you agree with her?"

"I don't know. It made sense at the time. I agreed with her because it felt like that to me. What do you think?"

"Treasure, I have a different opinion."

"Really? Please tell me."

"Based on Xavier's behavior pattern with different women, going on porn sites, using prostitutes, and looking for discreet encounters in chat rooms. On the contrary, you also mentioned he was doing nice things for you and obviously wasn't looking to leave you. It's highly possible that Xavier has some sort of dissociative disorder. This means being a possible addict, who can separate one part of his personality from the other, or he can psychologically remove himself from an experience he does not want to deal with and keep it in a separate compartment. I'm sure you have read of celebrities or well-known politicians' sexual secrets being exposed to the public. The response is often, 'How could he be so stupid?' Right? Treasure, when the same happens with a couple, the question of the hurt partner is often, 'How can he say he loves me if he has this other, secret life?'

"Oh my God, that's exactly how I questioned him. I asked how he could say he loves me all this time when he knows he's being deceitful. He still doesn't get it. The worst is not about having sex with those women; it's about him lying to me all those years, pretending to be someone he's not. That's fucking scary. It's like sleeping with a total stranger, and I had absolutely no idea who he truly is! He just doesn't get it!'"

"Yes, Treasure, and the answer to both questions is that acting out has two selves—his possible addict self and the healthy self—as well as the ability to keep them separate. His secret life is supported by lying to himself, you, and others; telling lies helps to cover his shame. The other tactic that he used was to pick fights with you. When you fought with him all those times, he would lie to himself that now he has a good reason to go to another woman. You also managed to realize that.

I forgot who called the two feelings of shame and guilt the "evil twins." I find it most clever and poignant, because our society at large still believes that shaming those who did bad deeds will motivate them to do good. It's the exact opposite; that is why you don't see addicts or inmates rush to change their maladaptive behaviors. Our jail system is still very much shame-based."

"I'm sure Xavier is no different. He feels uncomfortable when lying to you all this time, but he believes it is the lesser of two evils, fearing that telling the truth will get him into bigger trouble and make matters worse. By keeping his two parts separate, he allowed himself some false inner peace."

"My gosh, you're right. When I grilled him, he did mention something about feeling like two separate people, as if he has a split personality. I was so angry at the time. I thought he was lying and making up stories. But, Alicia, are you saying he could be addicted to sex or something else?"

"Well, after hearing your stories, I'm sure any therapist would request some sort of assessment. Do you know if his therapist has assessed him for any kind of disorder?"

"As a matter of fact, yes, Xavier told me he's getting his results back this week. I guess I'll find out when I get back to Shanghai."

"Well, okay, then. Let's wait and see. Oftentimes, there is some kind of pathology for someone behaving the way he is. Let's talk more when you know of the results. Treasure, we've been talking about Xavier quite a bit. Would you like to share with me about your mother's suicide? I think it's important that we talk about it."

"Of course, what can I say? It was, and is, extremely painful for me. It took me nearly a decade to heal. At least I *thought* I was healed, but now, suspecting I love a man who cannot love back, I believe I was so hurt by my mother's suicide that I subconsciously used my marriage to Xavier as an escape route for my pain, only to find myself revisiting it all over again."

"Are you saying you didn't love Xavier when you decided to marry him? You only used him to escape your pain?" I asked.

"No, Alicia, I'm not saying that at all. I'm saying the exact opposite," Treasure replied with a spark in her eyes. "I believe I loved him too much—I only loved the idealized him. I did not want to see the signs that his values are different from mine. Even before we started dating, there were rumors of him being unfaithful to Michellene. But I took that as mindless gossip, without further investigations. For instance, instead of insisting on finding out the true reasons for his divorce prior to falling in love with him, I secretly told myself that his ex-wife did not love him enough. This time would be different. If only I loved him more, he'd want to spend the rest of his life with me. I also thought as long as I loved him enough, he'd love me back. Not like my Mom. I always did what she asked of me; nevertheless, she left me without saying good-bye." Treasure slowly turned to look out of the window.

"Are you saying you're drawn to Xavier because you were not able to change your mother into the loving caretaker you needed as a child, and therefore you are attracted to the familiar type of emotionally unavailable man whom you can again try to change, through your love?"

"Maybe. I'm definitely considering that as a possibility in the foolish choices and actions I took in the past. Alicia, I help many clients that are exactly that. I'm not sure if I want to admit to what so many of us have—the disease of pleasing and loving too much! Like most girls, I've been taught as a child to be seen and not heard. I believe my parents had trained me well in that regard, particularly my Mom."

"How did your Mom train you to do that?" I asked.

"Oh, Alicia, it's a long story. I didn't have a close relationship with my father as a child. He showed me time and time again that he favored my older sister, Liz. He was seldom home, due to his work, and I don't remembering him ever spending alone time with Liz and me when he was home. I remember one time I had a quarrel with Liz. My Dad, without even finding out the truth, slapped me real hard across my face. It came so suddenly that I was in shock for a few minutes before my Mom came to my rescue. She scolded Dad for his action, and I guess from that moment on, I considered her my rescuer and protector. Subconsciously, I must have felt I had to please my mother in order to have her alliance. Oftentimes, my parents would manipulate us children, to make us be responsible for their emotions and relieve them of stress. Even one of my Mom's doctors would tell Liz and me not to fight because that would make our Mom sick and unhappy. I guess from an early age I was taught I am responsible for my mother's physical and emotional well-being. Nevertheless, I felt safe; at least I thought so at the time; until she decided to take her own life, and my whole world collapsed. I felt as if she abandoned me, to fend for myself alone!"

"I'm so sorry, Treasure. Did your Mom have depression?" I asked.

"Yes, we call it unipolar these days. I believe my Mom had unipolar or chronic depression for the longest time. I remember her bringing my sister and me to her endless visits to different doctors. She had trouble sleeping, and I remember her taking all kinds of medication. I was too young to know what they were for. As with many uncomfortable incidents that happened in our household, we never talked about it openly. As I told you earlier, the worst is that one of the doctors always blamed Liz and me for my mother's insomnia. I felt so responsible and guilty every time Liz and I had a quarrel. Intellectually, I knew it was only normal to have fights with your sibling, and yet we were always disciplined harshly for it. We weren't disciplined because our parents wanted us to respect each other and to deal with our emotions in a healthy manner; they wanted us to stop fighting because the arguments caused my mother's headaches and insomnia, and more visits to the doctors."

"It must be so confusing for you."

"Yes … among other feelings, like frustration, guilt, and anxiety. I never knew how my Mom would feel. Some days she seemed fine and upbeat, but as soon as she encountered stressful situations, she would then complain about her chronic headache and sleepless nights; particularly when she had fights with my Dad and Liz."

"Did they fight a lot?"

"I can't say for sure, it's such a long time ago; but I remember Mom always accused Liz of treating her friends better than her own blood. I also remember we would move every five years, and each time we moved, I knew Mom and Dad would fight."

"Why was that?"

"My Dad could be old-fashioned in some ways. I remember that when it came to borrowing money from the bank. My Mom was in charge of our finances, and her strategy was to have a mortgage and every five years sell the existing property to purchase another at a better location. My Dad didn't like the idea, so they argued. I remember one time it got so heated I was really frightened. I thought Mom was going to leave Dad."

"What happened?"

"It was one of those arguments about buying and selling properties. Liz and I were eavesdropping from my bedroom and discussing whether we should start packing and follow Mom. Of course she didn't leave Dad, but this was one of their 'moving house ritual' fights, until my Dad got a transfer to Nigeria."

"It seems to me you sided with your Mom at an early age?"

"I guess so. Probably because we were of the same gender and because I was not close to my Dad."

"What about your sister, Liz? Did she side with your Dad since she was Daddy's girl?"

"Actually no, not when we were young. I suppose at that age it's given that you will side with your mother. Anyway, we were too young to understand what's really going on."

"So, how would you describe your relations with your mother?"

"I'd say it was an illusion from the start. Knowing what I know now, I idealized my Mom the same way I idealized Xavier, and painted my Dad and Liz as villains in my world."

"Tell me more ..."

"I loved my Mom for the longest time and still do, but nobody's perfect. I miss her terribly, and it frightens me that her memory has slowly subsided in recent years. Don't get me wrong; I know she'll always be in my heart, but sometimes I don't remember what she looked like. I look at her photos often, so I remember what she used to be. As for my Dad, we had a heart-to-heart talk a decade before his passing. I got to know him better as a man, and not as the father I wanted him to be when I was young. It helps, you know, and I have had so much respect for him thereafter. I daresay we understood each other for the very first time.

"As I said earlier, I considered Mom my rescuer and protector, protecting me from my Dad's and Liz's bullying. I remember vividly that Mom used to spend time with me, telling me stories about her childhood and her relationship with her sister, my Aunt Jane. My Mom came from a well-to-do family. My grandfather was an antiques dealer in Shanghai; my grandmother died giving birth to my mother. Mom was the last of ten children, but many of her siblings died young; my Aunt Jane was thirteen years her senior. I'm not sure how Mom's mother's death impacted her, but I'm sure it is terrible to grow up without knowing who your mother was and never experiencing motherly love. My grandfather was never home, and Mom basically was cared for by her wet nurse.

"I could understand why she could be immature in dealing with love issues, life's adversities, and child rearing. I can't even begin to imagine how it must have made her feel, knowing her mother died giving birth to her. I am quite sure she blamed herself for her mother's death.

"I believe that unknowingly I also blamed myself for my mother's suicide. I felt I could have done more, to listen to her complaints more, to fix her, to make her well and happy again. I know I couldn't, but I still play the what-if game. What if I knew then what I know now, would she still be alive? Would I be able to help her?"

Tears welled up in Treasure's eyes, and I felt her pain and sorrow.

"Treasure, you're not responsible for your mother's death," I tried to remind her, knowing full well she knew that intellectually.

"Of course not, but I felt so helpless and frustrated for not being able to do anything! That's exactly how I felt when I first discovered Xavier's betrayal."

"Yes, Treasure, it makes sense. What else did your mother share with you?"

"Well, she told me how my Aunt Jane lied to my grandfather just after the war, that she was doing well in Hong Kong and urged him to send my Mom to Hong Kong, so she could look after her."

"Did your grandfather agree?"

"Yes, he did. He lost all his fortune overnight due to the liberation of the Communist Party. According to my Mom, he hated the Communist Party, because he blamed them for losing his wealth and social status. He refused to let my Mom enter their universities, although one of the universities had already accepted her. Instead, he sent her off to live with Aunty Jane. My Mom said she hated Hong Kong, because she so wanted to experience university life and have a tertiary education. I think this was one of her greatest regrets and shames. Also, my Aunt Jane was not doing as well as she led my grandpa to believe. She was working as a clerk in a textile factory, but her plan was to introduce my Mom to as many men as she could come across, hoping that with my Mom's beauty she could land herself a wealthy man who would look after them both."

"Was your father that man your Aunt Jane was hoping for?"

"No, far from it, my Dad wasn't well off when he met my Mom. My father's background is a total mystery to me. He never talked about it, and the bits and pieces I got from Mom were that he lost his mother at a young age, his father remarried, and after that it was your typical wicked stepmother story. So, my Dad left home when he was still a teenager, supported himself, and learned his trade in the textile industry. He was a textile engineer when they first met. Mom told me she thought he was after my Aunt Jane, because they were of similar age. Instead, my father had his eyes on Mom. She told me she didn't have much feeling for my father at first, but she knew he loved her and was reliable and dependable. I believe my Mom married my Dad for security and also to be rid of Aunty Jane's manipulation and control."

"Did your Mom tell you that?"

"Not in so many words, but I believe she did imply it. And then she told me that if I wanted to be happy, I ought to marry someone who loves me more than I love him. I really took her advice; therefore, all my relationships before Xavier were just that. And then I met him."

"What changed?"

"Mm, I suppose I fell for him hard. I really thought we had a balanced relationship, boy, was I wrong!"

"Why do you think your Mom gave you such advice?"

"I guess she needed someone to talk to, and I was just there. For crying out loud, she was only twenty when she married my Dad. I guess she was emotionally immature, but she was also a very attractive woman with a nice figure, and street smart too. I remember at her thirtieth birthday party, she wore this *qi-pao*, a traditional Chinese dress that showed off her curves and firm body. I was only eight at the time, and I thought she looked stunning. I remember secretly telling myself I was going to look like her when I grew old. It's funny how we think people in their thirties are old when we're kids." Treasure let out a laugh.

"It's sweet that you think of your Mom that way. You have very fond memories of your times together?"

"Yes. I always thought I had a pretty good childhood. Even now, I'll say that, but it's not all sweet and rosy. Certain experiences did have a negative impact on me. I realize it now."

"Tell me more."

"We were what you called a typical middle-class family. Dad was the breadwinner, and Mom was the main caretaker of the children. Unfortunately, like most parents in their generation, neither one of them knew that children need not only the basic things in life but, more importantly, unconditional love, affection, and emotional support.

"Having said that, I do know that they loved us children, and they did the best that they knew how. Nevertheless, I really don't remember spending time with my Dad when I was young, except in my primary school years; we had family outings on weekends regularly. My parents also took Liz and me to the cinemas a lot. I remember those times fondly. They didn't last long; something changed. One day our family car and full-time maid disappeared. As usual, nothing was told to us kids. From then on I always had to help my Mom out with housework, and when I had quarrels with Liz, she would tell me to be her good girl and let it go. She always had excuses for not confronting Liz, even though she knew I had been wronged. I remember feeling angry and frustrated, but I would tell myself, *I will be Mommy's good girl and let it slide, because I love her.* I wanted to be loved by her. She was my last hope; Liz was Daddy's girl. Subconsciously I must have believed I needed her alliance in order to survive. I suppose this has long been my way of feeling and expressing love.

"Well, as with most Asian families, it was important for us children to do well in school. My grades were actually good up until grade five, and after that—I don't know what happened. I was probably craving attention and hated being compared. Even negative attention is better than no attention at all! My parents always gave praise in front of friends about how well Liz did in school and how, although I'm not good in school, I'm my mother's good helper at home and I'm obedient. I remember my parents compared us a lot to each other and to other children as well. My grades just plummeted, to the point that I couldn't remain in the prestigious school both my sister and I attended, and I had to attend a private school near our apartment until my parents sent me off to boarding school in Canada. I believe I felt shamed by that, but when I got to Canada, I enjoyed the utter freedom, because it was not just about schoolwork. I learned to swim, dive, cycle, and play tennis and absolutely had a great time, because my deprived sportive nature finally was set free. In the process, I also learned that I wasn't the person my parents had told me I was; the part that I thought was unacceptable. I wasn't a complete academic disaster: I was good at the subjects I liked but when I'm uninterested in a subject, I would simply withdraw and even seemed unattached to whether I passed or failed. I always considered myself street smart. When I was a college freshman, my professor in persuasive skills told me I'd excel in marketing and sales. I took her advice to heart and later pursued a career in sales and marketing, before becoming a clinical counselor. Ironically, my sales and marketing career led me to meeting Xavier."

"I see. Was Liz always strong academically?"

"Yes and no. She got the grades to get into good schools, just as everyone expected of her. But I don't think she particularly enjoyed studying—or I should say the pressure everyone put on her. I'm sure she would have enjoyed it more had there not been so many expectations from my parents.

"She would get emotional, easily irritated around exam time, and I remember my Mom insisted we all tiptoe around her when she was studying, telling me not to disturb her. The fact that I had to behave in a certain way just because she was studying would annoy me. I thought to myself, *how unfair and unjust. She's not the only one who has to study.* Yet I had to accommodate her needs."

"You never shared how you felt with your parents?" I asked with concern.

"I did at first. Remember I told you earlier that Mom would find excuses for not confronting Liz? My father was seldom home, because of his work, and even when he was, I was sure he would side with Liz. It was my mother who told me to be *her good little girl* by not disturbing Liz. I so wanted to please my mother and to continue to get her love and affection, I thought I had to do what she asked of me."

"Treasure, do you feel when you were young that you were told to tend to your family's needs and feelings?"

Treasure thought for a while and said, "Definitely not consciously, but one thing is for sure, it's always been about everyone else's needs and feelings except mine." Tears welled up in Treasure's eyes once more. She tried to control her tears and continued, "I also remember something bizarre when we were still living in the old house. I think my Dad was still doing shift work at the time, and when he was on evening shifts, we had to tiptoe around the house; phones were all covered up, so the ring tone wouldn't wake him up. I guess there was no way to unplug the phone in those days. It was terrible; you could cut the tension with a knife anytime the phone rang or when we made a loud sound while Dad slept. My Mom was always anxious and tense. I remember one time my father came home with a bloody face, and nothing was mentioned. I remember being frightened by all the blood and was not given any explanation of what truly happened."

"For my parents, there were no accidents; even spilled milk was intentional. We were scrutinized and disciplined for breaking crystal glasses, dropping things on the expensive rugs, spilling liquid on the expensive sofas, etc. I remember one time we got severely punished when Liz had an accident. We were playing chase, and she fell and scraped her knees real bad, almost to the bone. I felt terrible, because I had initiated the chase, and seeing her bleeding and crying, I felt both guilty and sorry for her. Instead of giving support and comfort, my parents scolded us for playing chase, and we got punished on top of the scolding. They were harsher on me because I had initiated the game; nonetheless, we both got punished. I thought that was absolutely unjust and unloving."

"It seems to me you got blamed and punished for something natural and innocent for children. I can understand how you must have felt."

"Yes, anyway, I think I had long before developed into the rebel in the family. I remember feeling much anger every time I got unjustly punished and scolded. I guess the only way I could express my anger was to reject all the values my parents embodied, just or otherwise. And try to be different and opposite to everything and everyone in my family. I think I resented the fact that we looked so normal from the outside while I also had so much anxiety, frustration, anger, disappointment, hurt, and pain inside me. I wanted to scream at the top of my lungs how awful my family environment was at times, but no one else seemed to notice. As my Mom's depression got worse, she was more withdrawn, and I felt so alone battling with Dad and Liz. I believe the more they had me to be the one with the problem, the more I played along with the role."

"Yes, Treasure, it seems to me you shut off many of your feelings as a child. We need to explore further your relationships prior to meeting Xavier."

"Sure. I guess our time's up. Alicia, I'll Skype you when I'm back in Shanghai. Thank you."

As I watched Treasure leave, I couldn't help but feel a sense of loss. I missed her already.

Scene 4

HE WHO CAN'T LOVE BACK

Shanghai, PR China

"Hi, Alicia, can you hear me okay?"

"Yes, I can, but could you adjust your webcam? I can only see half your face."

"Is this better?" Treasure asked.

"Yes, thank you, and how are you, Treasure? How are things with Xavier?"

"We started couples therapy, and it feels strange. I'm reading a book his therapist recommended: *Forgiving Our Parents, Forgiving Ourselves* by Dr. David Stoop. He said in the book: "The well-adjusted family has found a balance between two seemingly contradictory dynamics: being close and being separate. It is balanced; it can adapt to change. Problems are handled on a family basis, not just an individual basis." I am now aware that I did not grow up in such a "well-adjusted" and safe environment. Stoop also referenced Laurie Ashner and Mitch Meyerson's book *When Parents Love Too Much*. It says, "If our environment is rigid, demanding, and conditional, however, we are forced to shape our behavior to fit the needs of others. We substitute our true self for a false self that is more acceptable to our parents, whose love and approval we need desperately. In essence we compromise who we really are, and become what our parents need us to be." I believe I also have learnt to do just that."

"Did you realize that from your couples' therapy or from the book?" I asked.

"It's mainly from the book. I don't particularly trust his therapist."

"Why is that?"

"Well, at first I thought she would have the life experience to help Xavier, because she is a bit older. I thought Xavier would feel more comfortable and safe with her. I don't see that happening; my gut feeling is there is something about her that I don't trust. I don't think she's sincere, and she's hiding something. Who knows? I could be wrong."

"I see. So it's not something in particular that she did?"

"Yes, it's only my perception and gut feeling, if you will. It doesn't really matter, because I don't think Xavier will continue with therapy much longer."

"But, Treasure, it's important for you to see a professional in order to make your relationship work.

You know he's going to hurt you again if he does not do his own internal work."

"I know that. You think I don't know that?" Treasure sounded annoyed.

"Okay, we can talk about this later. Is something else on your mind?" I didn't want to push her. Treasure must have her reasons.

"Remember I told you Xavier will be getting his personality assessment results?"

"Yes, I most certainly do."

"Yes, and I did. It's not good!"

I was hoping Treasure would continue after a long silence, but she did not.

"It's okay if you don't want to talk about it now," I exclaimed, thinking this must be the reason for Treasure to be short with me earlier.

"No, no, I *do* want to talk about it. His therapist used five different instruments to assess his personality. She said he has been diagnosed with four different traits— mid-range, not full-blown—of character disorders; he has antisocial and narcissistic traits; there is also clear evidence of a pattern of alcohol dependence. Well, I guess that makes your suspecting him of being an addict accurate. One of the assessments also profiled him as having an extreme need for excitement, and relationships are of little interest or value to him. Alicia, I feel devastated, overwhelmed, scared, and totally dejected by the news. I feel so helpless!"

"Oh, Treasure. I'm so, so sorry to hear that."

There was another long silence.

Finally, Treasure related, "All instruments implicated he presents as an emotionless individual, and that he carries a bit of a grudge. A precise metaphor for his emotional state is an iceberg. He's more comfortable being a follower than a leader, a technical person than a manager. So his career choice requires him to play a role outside of his comfort zone. No wonder every time he has a pre-opening project he's all stressed out and distant. The assessment results also say he avoids emotional exchange and is unable to relate to women as other than sexual objects. That's why he has no problem exploiting them. Shit, it all makes sense now."

"What all makes sense?" I asked.

"His behavior, Alicia; it all makes sense to me now. Furthermore, the results suggest that he has rejected any feminine characteristics in his personality and that he dominates women as a way of feeling powerful. It is highly unlikely he has the sense of self to feel equal in a marital relationship. His need for excitement and sexual dalliance portrays him as using women and circumstances to avoid pain and help him to feel alive, at least for a short while. His self-concept is quite undeveloped and superficial; his relationships must bolster his sense of worth. Uh, I really know how to pick them, don't I?" Treasure stared straight at me with despair.

"Did you talk to him about the results?" I asked with concern.

"Yes, and he said he feels very depressed and hopeless. He also says if he's not going to get better what's the point of doing therapy. I think he's already made up his mind to give up. I now know why he never fought for Michellene, Sabrina and Vanessa—and now me, us. He never wanted a relationship to begin with; he was only using us women to make him feel alive. Yes, he's a taker; it's his narcissistic traits. I can see now, ever since we got married, I seldom feel love or affection from him because he's a man that's unable to love. All the nice things I thought he did for me out of love, he did for himself and others to see; it's all superficial. He wanted people to think he's a loving husband, but he knows he's not. He's a great pretender. He's definitely the contaminator in our marriage, but I know I am the contributor, because I allowed him to contaminate our relationship all these years. I was seeing him with colored glasses. I loved a man who cannot love back, and I was too afraid to face the truth!"

Back Stage

SELF-REFLECT AND AWARENESS:

1) Are there things happening in your life right now that you are ignoring to see and/or refusing to examine?

2) Are you also pretending to be someone you are not only to get someone's love and affection?

3) In what ways are you disrespecting your own feelings, desires and needs?

4) What is the truth that you are refusing to see?

5) What are you ready to admit to now?

6) What are you not confronting and wish to see?

7) Are you someone that uses sex, drugs, alcohol, work, or other addictive behaviors to regulate your own negative emotions and/or inadequacies?

8) What is your childhood story?

9) Are you someone who also learned to shut off many of your justifiable feelings as a child?

10) Are you someone who learned to substitute your true self for a false self that is more acceptable to your parents?

11) Did you manage to compromise who you really are, and become what your parents need you to be?

ACT II

The Beginning of the Journey (A Slow Awakening)

A person does not have to be behind bars to be a prisoner. People can be prisoners of their own concepts and ideas; they can be slaves to their own selves.

Maharaji

Scene 5

WITHOUT BOUNDARIES

Shanghai, China

Xavier stood at the end of the waiting line, seeming calm and patient, with a bouquet of flowers in hand. Treasure spotted him easily, because he was the only non-Asian there. He looked well; obviously he'd been looking after himself. He didn't look remorseful.

"Welcome back, my Weibs. Thank you for coming back." As Xavier held Treasure in his arms and handed her the flowers, she saw tears in his eyes.

"Did you think I was not coming back? I never said I was not coming back." Instead of being touched by this remark—and the flowers and the pet name—Treasure appeared irritated.

"I was afraid you weren't, but I am happy you are back now. Weibs, I promise I will not commit adultery ever again. I will not visit porn sites or chat rooms, and I will be a devoted, committed, and faithful spouse to you, as you have always been to me." Treasure felt indifferent to the meaningless words Xavier uttered to her as their chauffer-driven car sped off from the Pudong airport.

The following months with Xavier were unpredictable, and Treasure had no idea that she was yet to experience some of the most scary emotional roller-coaster rides in her life.

"Hi, Treasure, how have you been?" I asked as we Skyped.

"Do you mean physically or mentally?" Treasure asked with a smile.

"You still keep your sense of humor. That's good news." I returned her smile.

"Well, to be honest, a lot has happened since we last talked."

"Okay, maybe you could start by sharing with me whether you and Xavier have made any changes."

"I don't think so. Despite individual, group, and couples' therapy, he's still not sharing much or answering any of my questions about his sexual behaviors, and God knows what else he's not telling me. He wants everything back to normal, and that I should really trust him, now that he's apologized once in a letter and another time in an e-mail. He keeps on saying group therapy is not helping him and that he's not getting the support he needs. I believe it's his way to wiggle out of any existing therapy. He has shown no desire to change for the better."

"I'm sorry to hear that, Treasure."

"So is I. Alicia, I've been doing a lot of soul-searching lately. I am determined to find out my role in our relationship."

"Have you learned anything useful that you'd like to share with me?"

"I believe so, and it's not pretty." Treasure took a deep breath. "I saw the dark side of me, as Carl Jung would say, the shadows. I believe I contributed to our existing relationship because I had no boundaries—loving too much."

Hearing that comment, I couldn't help but drift off to my own predicament at home once again.

"Alicia ... Alicia, can you hear me?"

"Yes, Treasure. Sorry, it's bad connection. Yes, I believe we did touch on boundaries in previous sessions."

"Remember you told me we need to explore my relationships before meeting Xavier?" Treasure asked timidly.

"Yes, I do," I replied with anticipation.

"Alicia, I also remember you telling me that as a child I learned to shut off a lot of my feelings. It's highly possible, but after a lot of self-reflection and observation of my own behavior the past months, I believe I may also have developed a couple of defense mechanisms against my uncomfortable feelings."

"What defense mechanisms are you referring to?"

"I believe I often use denial and control as tools of self-protection. Remember we discussed in our sessions that my Dad often sided with my sister, Liz, and unbeknownst to my Mom, she manipulated me to have me do what she wanted?"

"Yes, Treasure, I do remember."

"Well, I guess all those times when I felt wrongly accused or misunderstood by my parents, I was led to believe that I wasn't good enough to be really loved. No matter what I did, I couldn't seem to get their approval or acceptance. I remember they would use really harsh words and name calling at times to show how disappointed they were with me. I don't remember witnessing them using the same discipline methods with Liz. I don't doubt that most likely there was transference on their part; nevertheless, I believe it impacted me negatively in a big way. I hate to admit that I also used similar methods with Xavier when we were fighting or when I tried to express my feelings of disappointment in his behaviors. He never shared with me that his father verbally abused him when he was a child; I only found that out recently from Michellene. No wonder I triggered so much hurt emotions every time I swore or called him names."

"Hmm, that's definitely very insightful." I can't say I disagreed with Treasure.

"Wait, Alicia, it gets better. I was thinking back to all my past relationships with men. I had the tendency to attract men that somehow tolerated my thinking they needed to be educated for the better. I remember my one boyfriend of six years in Toronto. Park was the youngest of six children from a very traditional Korean family. I would say he was mama's boy. At the time he was twenty-six and still living with his eldest sister's family. He worked part-time and was struggling to finish college. His mother would do his laundry and cook for him. You know what I did? Probably it was jealousy combined with a sense of self-righteousness, but I would criticize him for being dependent and having no ambition. Little did I realize then that probably his mother needed him around more than he did her. I tried to break up with him many, many times, but to no avail, because he was absolutely obsessed with me. And I was obsessed with his love and protection. One time I even needed his rescue. It was definitely a dysfunctional relationship. I know I hurt him real bad, and I am certainly not proud of it. But then again, I was too young to know any better. I truly thought I was doing the right thing by him and us."

"Thank you for sharing that with me, Treasure. It takes courage to admit that you also can wrong someone unintentionally. But what do you mean by you needed his rescue?"

Treasure raised her eyebrows and replied, "Oh, that."

"Yes?"

"Hmm, I remember ..." After a long pause, Treasure continued. "Park and I used to live downtown in the same building but in separate apartments. After several unsuccessful breakups and one that involved police arresting him for harassment, I decided to move out and share a house uptown with the sister of one of his good friends. She was living by her lonesome and wished to have a housemate, and I thought that with her in the house, it would be more difficult for Park to harass me further, but ..."

"Did the plan work?" I interrupted Treasure.

"Yes, it did, until her parents visited one summer. My housemate and her mother were upstairs, and her father and I were in the lounge room watching television. That's when he made sexual passes at me and made all sorts of derogative remarks about my body parts and how smooth my skin was. As I was feeling immobilized, I was saved by Park's phone call."

"What happened?" I asked with a sense of urgency.

"Something very strange happened when I got on the phone with him. Mind you, my roommate's father was still nearby, so I only answered Park's questions with a brief yes or no. When he asked how I was doing, I replied with a short no and then, out of the blue, Park just came out and asked me a question that even till this day I had no idea how he knew to ask it."

"What did he ask you?"

"Well, he asked me if my roommate's father did something inappropriate."

"How could he have known?" Like Treasure, I was puzzled by his question.

"Yes exactly! We had not spoken with each other for quite some time, and I thought that could finally be the end of our relationship. But as soon as he asked me that, I couldn't help myself, and I replied yes. He immediately offered to pick me up from the house. I left that evening and stayed with Park till my housemate's parents left Toronto. But by then we were romantically involved again. I had no one to turn to but him, and I'm glad he was there for me. For that, I'm forever grateful!" Tears welled up in Treasure's eyes.

"You never managed to find out how he knew?" I continued to question Treasure.

"No, it was so long ago. I was still in college. But I did ask him. I think his answer was not to my satisfaction; otherwise, I would have remembered. I don't know why I did not pursue the truth further. Gee, it just dawned on me that that's my pattern ..."

"What pattern?" I interrupted.

"My pattern of getting scared of finding out the truth."

"How old were you then?"

"I was nineteen. I felt absolutely terrified, helpless, and alone. I was confused and did not set boundaries to protect myself from my roommate's father, but I used Park instead."

"Treasure, I am glad Park did come to your rescue. But you could not have foreseen the behavior of your roommate's father."

"No, of course not, but I could have confronted him head-on. I was too afraid to, because I believed that neither his wife nor his daughter would believe my story. It was my word against his. Even one of my classmates doubted me when I shared that with her."

"What happened?" I asked.

"She asked me if I could have mistaken. Yeah, right. As if I could have mistaken his hard-on being pushed behind me as something else. I was absolutely livid with her for not believing me. Not only did it trigger all those times that my parents did not believe what I said, but I also felt so helpless and guilty that I used Park, when I clearly communicated that I wished to end the relationship."

"Treasure, I believe you are too critical of yourself. I believe that incident triggered your childhood fears and insecurities, but you were right not to confront him, because most likely they would side with him, even if they knew you were telling the truth. As for using Park, I disagree with you; it was he who called you. You needed help; he was there. But are you saying you failed to break up with Park yet again because after the incident you felt obliged to rekindle your romantic relationship?"

"Yes, that's exactly what I'm saying. I felt I was using him, so I had to pay him back with my love. We were so enmeshed, not knowing how to set boundaries with each other. Of course, that's not love. I know that now."

"Treasure, you were involved in a very scary situation; there's no shame in getting help, even if it's from someone you wanted to break up with."

"Thank you, Alicia. I appreciate that. But more importantly, I realized that I'm still that scared little girl. I believe my anger at Xavier's betrayal is directed more at myself—my prolonged unawareness of the problems in the relationship, my accepting the unacceptable and not challenging things sooner, my not setting boundaries to protect myself. Furthermore, I am angry at my incompetence in helping my mother at her darkest hour. I feel as if I've let myself down." Tears started to roll from Treasure's eyes once more.

I so wanted to reach across and hold her in my arms, although I know I had to keep my boundaries as her counselor. Fortunately, we were Skyping. I said, "Yes, Treasure, you'll find that your self-criticism may be the hardest obstacle to overcome before you can forgive Xavier."

"What do you mean? I don't follow."

"Treasure, you have to forgive yourself first, before you can forgive another, whether it is Xavier, your parents, Liz, or anyone else. Don't forget, you are dealing with a number of losses—to name just a few, the loss of the dream relationship you thought you had with Xavier, the loss of trust with his betrayal. Above all, I don't think you have really processed the loss caused by your mother's suicide. Your inner child needs your compassion and not more criticism."

"Yes, Alicia, I know I have to forgive myself first." Treasure interrupted me with a sense of sorrow, and then she abruptly changed to another topic. "Who knows? Maybe Xavier had a point about me trying to change him. Actually, why is the idea of changing our partners for the better so enticing for us women? If you ask me, it's strange. How can you love someone and yet want them to change? I guess we are all illusionists. Alicia, I believe in some ways we are all scared shitless to choose a road of maturity that we have to follow alone."

"Hmm, Treasure, these are all interesting questions. I suppose it comes from our society's beliefs and religion. They all teach us to help those who cannot help themselves. We are also taught that it is our obligation and duty to respond with compassion and generosity when someone is in trouble."

"Now, I'm not saying all these motives can explain why millions of women choose men who are disrespectful, cruel, insensitive, disengaging, emotionally unavailable, addicted, deceitful, and, most of all, unable to be loving and caring. I've come across some women that can behave in similar ways or worse. But I would say this—women who do not know how to set boundaries and who love too much tend to make these choices out of a driving need to control those closest to them. Somehow, that need to control others originates in a childhood during which many overwhelming emotions are experienced, like fear, anger, unbearable tension, guilt, shame, feeling sorry for others and for self. A child growing up in such an environment would be wracked by these emotions to the point of being unable to function unless she developed ways to protect herself. Unfortunately, Treasure, you are correct: most of the time, your tools for self-protection are what you mentioned earlier—*denial*, and another powerful subconscious motivation, *control*. Of course, it's a *false* sense of control."

"Yes, Alicia, I absolutely agree with you. Furthermore, I believe I was indeed living in an environment that was full of severe tension, guilt, shame, anger, and fear. I also believe my parents had somehow subconsciously assigned me the roles of caretaker, rebel, and scapegoat. As long as I was the problem child, they didn't have to look closely at their own issues. Sadly, I also learned not to look closely at my own issues. I must now stop using the same kind of destructive tools for self-protection that I learned as a child. I see it now."

Scene 6

DARKNESS BEFORE LIGHT

Sydney, NSW, Australia

The ten-hour business–class flight from Shanghai was pleasant enough for Treasure. She managed to get some sleep in the night and landed in the early hours in beautiful Sydney. She was looking out the plane window, feeling excited. She could not wait to see Daisy; the last time the two shared her "Xavier saga" was five months ago.

As soon as the automatic door slid open, there she was, a small-framed woman with her signature short spiky hair. Treasure sometimes wondered why Daisy wouldn't dye her gray hair; she would look much younger. It was a bit masculine for Treasure's taste, but she always thought Daisy wore it well, and her good fashion sense helped.

Treasure first met Daisy when she gave up her career in Hong Kong, not long after her mother's suicide, to join Xavier in Sydney. Grigio, Daisy's husband, was the restaurant manager at the hotel, where Xavier was his direct boss. Grigio was tall, dark, and handsome in his younger years. In later years he developed a big gut and walked like a prematurely old man.

Treasure and Daisy did not hit off immediately; one reason was that they never spent one-on-one time—it was always the four of them. A few years later, when Xavier got his first transfer to Shanghai, Treasure stayed behind for another six months to sort out their household affairs. It was then that the pair spent much time together and bonded.

Treasure was so happy to see Daisy that she picked her up with both arms as they hugged. "Hey, you're looking good, girl!" Daisy remarked.

"Well, thanks. Considering what I'm going through, right? Hey, you don't look too bad yourself!" They laughed out loud like two teenagers as they drove away in Daisy's red-hot four-door Mini-Cooper.

"Okay, I'm really hungry. You need to feed me as soon as I've checked into the hotel. You know how I get when my sugar level is low."

"Yes, my dear, I remember it well. Hey, but eat just a little, because Grigio has cooked up a feast for you."

"Great! You know how much I love his cooking."

By the time they arrived at the restaurant near Daisy and Grigio's flat, it was already well into lunchtime. Treasure found herself gulping down her first glass of sauvignon blanc with an empty stomach. She started updating Daisy on her "Xavier saga," and tears filled her eyes when the subject of her mother's suicide came up. Daisy was sipping her wine slowly and unmoved, listening to Treasure without interruptions or questions. She sat quietly.

Meanwhile, Treasure downed her second glass, this time with a half dozen oysters. She felt a bit tipsy as soon as she had the third glass of white upon arriving at Daisy and Grigio's flat. By then, it was almost dinnertime, and the last thing Treasure remembered was that she was sobbing uncontrollably into Daisy's bosom when she heard her say, "Treasure, you really need to get over your mother's death."

The TV was still running and all the lights were on when Treasure found herself half-naked in her hotel bed. As she slowly opened her sleepy eyes, she felt the famished sensation of an empty stomach, which was soon followed by her first thought: "What did I do that they didn't feed me?"

Treasure could not bear the question. She reached over to the bedside table and picked up the chocolate wafer of Tim Tam she had somehow purchased from the hotel kiosk shortly before they departed to the restaurant. As Treasure slowly peeled off the bar of Tim Tam, the same question crept back into her head. Then the answer came: "I must have done something terrible; that's why they didn't feed me." Tears started to come while she was still chewing the bar of Tim Tam, and suddenly she felt a slight pain in her forehead. Treasure tried to ignore it, thinking it could be a hangover, but somehow she knew it was a different kind of pain. She finished her Tim Tam and still had no clue how she ended up in her hotel room. She couldn't remember a thing, but she thought maybe Grigio had taken her home. She got out of bed and walked into the living area of the suite; she looked around slowly to search for clues, and when she caught sight of her handbag lying in the middle of the coffee table, she realized it wasn't Grigio or Daisy who took her home. She saw the way the handbag was positioned; it was too familiar. She knew only she could have laid it that way. Suddenly, the sharp pain knocked on her forehead again, and Treasure proceeded to the bathroom mirror. She brushed up her fringe, and there it was, a tiny lump just above her right eyebrow. As she was feeling sleepy and groggy, Treasure decided to go back to bed and let the night's worries rest.

It was only the next morning when Treasure realized the small swollen lump from last night had now extended to a large black eye. More questions arose: *How did I manage to get back to my room? How could they not let me stay at their place when I was a mess? How could they not bring me back to my hotel? What if I had an accident and lost all consciousness? How could they? What happened? What did I do?*

Scene 7

FACING HER SHADOW

Brisbane, Queensland, Australia

"Yes, I can see how serious it is. The black and blue underneath your eye. So what really happened?" I asked with concern.

"I really don't know, Alicia."

"What do you mean?" I was puzzled by Treasure's reply.

"Well, I guess I used denial again to block the hurtful feelings and all, afraid to find out the truth again! I believe I felt shame as well."

"Tell me more."

"When I saw Daisy the next day, she told me I was in hysterics and that Grigio could not handle it, because it triggered his childhood horror. I guess she blamed me for seeing him like that. She said I was so angry I broke one of their kitchen chairs. Grigio's father was both physically and verbally abusive toward his mother and him. His father once put his handgun against Grigio's temple. I suppose how I acted reminded him of the trauma he experienced as a child. Daisy said he fled to the sunroom and left her in the kitchen to fend me off."

"Why did she say she had to fend you off?" I asked in dismay.

"Yes, as if I were a monster that could hurt them. Not a word you would use for someone you've known for a decade who is supposedly your best friend. Don't get me wrong; I'm sure it must have been frightening. God knows I've never seen that side of myself. I didn't realize I could harbor so much anger that I had the strength to break a solid wooden chair. The thing is I don't remember what happened, not a thing."

"Other than you're crying in Daisy's bosom?"

"Yes, that's the last thing I remember before my dark side emerged."

"How did you get your black eye, then?"

"Well, that's a mystery. Daisy told me it was when I leaned backward and fell from my chair. I then was rolling back and forth on the floor and crying uncontrollably. It got so loud that their downstairs neighbor complained. I guess they felt embarrassed by the drama and didn't know how to handle the situation," Treasure explained.

"What are your feelings about all that?"

"I feel anger, hurt, and shame. What hurt me most was that I didn't expect Daisy to be so unempathetic.

I felt betrayed and abandoned in my hour of need. Of course, I am ashamed of my shadow behavior. I do take full responsibility for that."

"Yes, Treasure, you have every right to feel those feelings. I am not saying your irrational behavior was triggered by Daisy's last words to you; however, her words were disrespectful and unempathetic. You don't just tell someone they ought to get over their emotions; in doing so, you're indirectly telling them their emotions are not important," I explained.

"Thank you, Alicia, for pointing that out to me. While we were having lunch the day after the incident, she invited me back to their place for dinner, but she said Grigio told her to convey that he didn't want me there if I behaved the same way as the night before."

"Hmm ... go on."

"I then asked her why we didn't have dinner the night before, and her reason was that I kept on asking to leave. Alicia, her story just doesn't add up, and I was too ashamed to pursue the truth further. I apologized and offered to pay for the broken chair. Daisy declined my offer, but I don't remember her making any comment about my apology."

"How did the second dinner attempt go?"

"When I arrived at their place, Grigio came to the door, and I immediately apologized for my scary behavior and also offered to pay for the damaged chair. He declined and acted it was nothing, but I knew it wasn't nothing."

"Treasure, would you like to explore what motivated you to go all-out with Daisy and Grigio at their apartment?"

"I'm not sure, Alica. It's not as if I planned it intentionally."

"I understand, Treasure. Nonetheless, it's important to explore your subconscious, yes?'

Treasure looked at me in dismay and finally she replied after a long pause …

"I suppose so."

"Good, so what do you think motivated you to be utterly vulnerable that evening?"

"I really have no idea. Obviously, it was done under the influence of alcohol; maybe subconsciously I wanted to test the loyalty of their friendship? It is clear to me now that I chose the wrong people to purge too much, and it backfired on me!"

"Yes Treasure, I must commend you on your self-awareness; and have you heard of the term *floodlighting*?

Treasure thought for a while, shook her head and I continued to explain.

"In her book *Daring Greatly* Brene Brown mentioned two forms of oversharing in our culture. One form is what she called *floodlighting*. She explained that the intentions behind this kind of sharing are multifaceted and often include what you just suspected your subconscious did—loyalty and tolerance testing in a relationship."

Treasure stared at me with a blank look, so I decided to continue …

"Nevertheless, it is vital to exercise self-compassion. Treasure, you definitely have to give yourself a break when you share too much with someone that wasn't able to hold space for you. When you mentioned earlier that Grigio had an abusive father, and I'm not even sure what's Daisy's story; it doesn't really matter. It's clear to me that they weren't able to hold space for you when you hit them with the floodlight. Clearly there were judgment, and instead of getting the empathy and connectedness you hoped for, disconnection occurred. Therefore, I wanted you to talk this out in the open so it won't compound your shame further, does it makes sense?"

"Yes Alicia, it makes a lot of sense. Thanks so much for that, I had no idea that I was *floodlighting* Daisy and Grigio. But, are you saying *floodlighting* is not really vulnerability then?"

"Great question, Treasure; yes, according to Brene Brown, it is not. Not when you use it to test loyalty of a friendship, even without you knowing consciously then."

"May I ask, what is a healthy way to share vulnerability then?"

"Mm, good question Treasure; I suppose the key is to know the difference between using vulnerability and just being vulnerable. They are not the same. Another rule of thumb is to know your own boundaries around what you share and what you don't share and be mindful of your intentions and whether the behavior is appropriate. It's better to work through your vulnerabilities with a professional before you share with the people you love and you think they could hold the space for you. It requires a lot of trust, reciprocal sharing, empathy, compassion and so you know that they've earned the right to hear them. Basically, people that you've cultivated a deep relationship with that can bear the weight of your story or behavior."

"Yes Alicia, but I thought that's what I had with Daisy and Grigio? We were friends for a decade? Well, I suppose with Daisy, not so much Grigio?"

"Treasure, think back, how much of your stories have you shared with them and have they always reciprocated the sharing? Were they empathetic? Did you not tell me once that Daisy is quite judgmental?"

"Yes, yes, Alicia … you're right, there weren't much reciprocal sharing in the past, Daisy enjoyed listening to my stories but shared little about hers. Gosh, I had no idea Alicia … gosh, I feel so violated and angry at myself now."

"Treasure, maybe it's a good opportunity to practice self-compassion and forgiveness?"

"What? To forgive myself or them?"

"Both, Treasure, it's always about us, not them! You can't forgive anyone without first forgiving self."

Scene 8

LURKING SHADOWS

Shanghai, China

Things went from bad to worse. It has been months since Xavier moved into their guest room. There was hardly any physical contact, except for the occasional hand-holding. On a good day, Treasure could concentrate on her own daily routine and try to figure out how to salvage this relationship, but on a bad day she couldn't help but keep pursuing Xavier for more "Q&A" that he simply was not able to anticipate or provide.

On the evening of yet another corporate event, Treasure put on her usual supportive "corporate wife's mask" and attended the party with Xavier. As she was enjoying a conversation with a stranger, suddenly, Treasure saw Xavier's ex-employee who was a good friend of Sasha, another woman that Treasure believed Xavier was sleeping with. Treasure immediately felt uncomfortable, and, under the influence of alcohol, she fell into a deep spell of humiliation and anger.

On their way home, Treasure was boiling with anger, feeling humiliated, rejected, and alone. Treasure found her getting more and more vocal with Xavier.

"You never loved me, did you? It's all a lie; the whole marriage was a sham. I only realize now that you're a true user, and you just take and take." Treasure kept following Xavier to the guest room, when he turned to her and exclaimed, "You're drunk. And stop asking me all these questions that I have no answer to." Xavier found Treasure kept at his tail, and he felt helpless. Instinctively, he decided to lock the door behind him, and that was the worst thing he could have done at that instant.

Treasure did not let up; she kept on cursing Xavier while pounding on the door, demanding Xavier to open up. It was all in vain. Then suddenly, Treasure heard soft voices saying, "No, don't do it. You know they're movie props to make it look easy. You're going to hurt yourself." Then another voice came through: "Who is this person that is trying to kick the door down?"

"Oh, Treasure! Did you hurt yourself?" I questioned without thinking.

"Luckily not, looking back, I could have hurt my knees real bad. Mind you, I was wearing heels as well. Alicia, I don't know what came over me. I suppose I was so overwhelmed by my emotions that I lost sanity in a split second. It's as if I had an out-of-body experience; I was outside looking in as I was attempting to kick the bedroom door down in slow motion. I don't even know what I was trying to achieve. I can't be sure, but I believe I stopped at two kicks. Then I collapsed by the door, sobbing in indescribable pain, and felt utterly numb at the same time." Her head lowered and she was staring at the floor.

"Treasure, it's not uncommon that when you're in immense pain, your spirit tends to break away from your physical form. It's a form of self-protection, if you will. I'm sure that is what you experienced as an out-of-body experience."

"Yes, that must have been it. I recall having a similar sensation when I witnessed my mother's corpse at the morgue soon after her death."

"I'm so sorry, Treasure! And then what happened?"

"Well, I'm not sure how long I cried outside the door before Xavier finally opened the door and let me in. I just went straight to the bed, curled up like a baby, and cried. I kept on muttering that he never loved me and that our marriage was all a lie. He just sat there in his armchair like a stunned mullet. I knew then he's incapable of giving love and empathy. As a matter of fact, I'm sure at that moment he perceived me as weak and drunk. I'm a reflection of him—the part of him that he finds unacceptable."

"Treasure, why would you jump to this conclusion?"

"Alicia, I've not told you what transpired the following weeks."

"Oh, my apologies, please go on."

"Again he pretended nothing happened, and we never talked about that night. However, a string of incidents soon followed, and for a period of a month I felt threatened by his demeanor. I had to double-lock my bedroom door and put a chair against it, because he has a master key to all the hotel rooms."

"Why? What happened that made you so afraid of him?" I asked with great concern.

"Every time I badgered him with more questions about his deceitful ways, and he couldn't reply, I would make snide remarks about his character, and an evil grin would show on his face."

"Did you confront him with this?" I asked.

"Yes, of course. I was frightened that he might harm me physically, but I did not show it. Instead, I confronted him straight on; I guess that provoked him even further. It was on his sixty-fourth birthday that he announced he was quitting therapy. I expressed my disappointment to no avail, and it was during another heated argument that I saw *contempt* on his face. I knew instantly I have to leave Xavier for my own safety, sanity, and dignity. Alicia, soon after that dark evening, I read in his journal that he felt helpless and sad, that it's hopeless. He said he had thought I was so together, and after that incident I totally disappointed him."

"Hmm, is this the first time he saw you break down?" I asked.

"Yes, that's for sure, and I'd say this is also my first, not counting the incident at Daisy and Grigio's place when I blacked out and couldn't remember what exactly happened."

"Well, Treasure, the fact is that you're a strong, competent, effective woman. But don't forget, you're no different than everyone else; you also have bad days, particularly under these circumstances. Unfortunately, I agree with you. It seems to me when you dared to express your vulnerability, instead of giving you love and emotional support, Xavier showed disgust and contempt. It seems to me he does not see you as another human being separate from him, who also has needs and feelings of her own. As we've explored in our previous sessions, he's a possible misogynist incapable of giving love. Now that he's quit therapy, how's he to learn the skills of giving and receiving love?"

"Yes, I know it's not good. No wonder he didn't do anything when I was in fetal position crying. He was shocked to see me totally broken down before him. It seems he was saying to me, *who are you to break down? Who are you not to be strong to take care of things and suck up everything? What am I to do now? You're supposed to be the strong one!* Yes, Alicia, ever since I found him out, he tends to say he needs me more than he says he loves me. I feel defeated and tired; however, for the first time in my life, I know I have to face my fears and reality even though it is not what I wanted. I have to divorce Xavier to gain back my dignity and integrity." Treasure looked straight at me and our eyes locked.

"Treasure, you don't need to decide now, as long as you know you are safe. The wound is still very raw, and you need to be patient and compassionate with yourself and let yourself grieve and heal. You'll know for sure what to do when you can think clearer; I'm sure of that."

"Well, Alicia, it's good to know you have such faith in me." Treasure gave me her invigorating smile while tears still filled her eyes.

Back Stage

SELF-REFLECT AND AWARENESS:

1) What healthy or unhealthy defense mechanisms you have acquired to soothe your uncomfortable feelings?

2) What kind of childhood environment did you grow up in?

3) As Robert Holden said, "We bring to the relationship what we know." So, what did you bring to your relationship that is not serving you?

4) Are you one of those people who have also used *floodlighting*?

ACT III

Wisdom Born of Pain

Life will bring you pain all by itself.
Your responsibility is to create joy.

Milton Erickson

Scene 9

MYTHS ABOUT LOVE

Brisbane, Queensland, Australia

Here I am, a glass of bubbles in hand on my front porch, thinking of Treasure's case and my own relationships. I'm slowly coming to terms with how we all want the same things in life—importance, acceptance, and, most of all, to love and be loved. Yet billions of us on earth are just not getting it. Those that do are of the minority. Divorce rates have risen sky-high in the past decade, and the more technology we invent, the less we feel connected to one another, particularly our loved ones. You can't help but ask yourself, *what is really going on?*

In her book *Everybody Marries the Wrong Person,* Christine Meinecke mentions that the conventional wisdom about romantic relationships remains unquestioned. I cannot help but agree. Fairy tales like "Sleeping Beauty" set girls up for total disappointment with the notion that girls are helpless victims who, because they are beautiful, Prince Charming will eventually come to rescue. They teach that basically there's one right person for everyone. Shakespeare's *Romeo and Juliet* teaches how they had to go through pain and suffering in order to be together. Nobody teaches our young that healthy love does not hurt and that certainly nobody needs to kill oneself for another in the name of love.

Further perpetuating misconceptions and myths can only lead us down the path of relationship and marital dissatisfaction. I would like to reiterate a few of what Meinecke identifies as false beliefs:

1) *It's better to be unhappy with someone than to be alone.* The core of this belief is the fear of having no one to turn to in times of overwhelming trauma or financial ruin. Furthermore, this attitude perpetuates another belief, that being alone is something to be avoided. We fear the loss of companionship and loneliness.

   No doubt, partners can be at their best when working together toward common goals as a team and equal partnership. However if the relationship is unbalanced and dysfunctional, the only self-care way to live is to be alone.

2) *As lifelong partners, we are supposed to fulfill each other's wants and needs.*

It may seem harmless, but Meinecke mentioned that this myth cannot be separated from its roots—the lopsided belief that wives are expected to fulfill their husbands' wants and needs. It seems to provide justification for abuse of women. As we all know, even in the twenty-first century, some societies continue to criminalize wives' refusing sex to their husbands, tolerate public floggings, and ignore honor killings of women. Women are perceived as properties and are not identified as equals.

In my practice I have seen the majority of my clients making similar mistakes of holding their spouse responsible for satisfying their wants and needs (both men and women are guilty). Heck, I am guilty of that too.

Meinecke points out that the key concept is that emotionally mature adults take responsibility for fulfilling their own needs and wants.

3) *Love cures loneliness.*

No doubt, courtship can lead to love and companionship. Unfortunately, our expectations mislead us when we believe that the love of a romantic partner will banish our loneliness and sense of inadequacy. My many clients (both men and women) have experienced feeling lonely while with their significant other, and they don't understand why. Oftentimes, they blame their spouses.

- He doesn't like to talk about his emotions.
- He doesn't listen.
- He doesn't care about my concerns and the children.
- He doesn't know what I need.
- She doesn't pay attention to me.
- She doesn't support me.
- She doesn't understand me.
- I could never live up to her expectations.

I totally agree with Meinecke; the issue is not with the spouse. It is with the lonely one's distorted expectations.

A man often wishes his partner could be like a teammate, participating with him in his hobbies, be it in sports, games, or other activities of mutual interest. He may feel disappointed when his partner is not interested in hiking, detailing motorcycles, or cars. By the same token, a woman often wishes for a partner who could be like a girlfriend, also enjoying empathetic conversations or shopping.

With unmet unrealistic expectations like the above, no wonder we feel disconnected from our partners. Bear in mind that individuals often have different preferences for getting companionship needs met; disappointments are inevitable. It is exactly because we don't wish others to experience feeling disappointment in us that we live in fear and lie, or have the disease to please and fear of saying no.

It is important to learn and to teach our young that it is vital to take responsibility for meeting our own needs in order to be emotionally mature adults. It is our choice to be generous and loving to our partners; therefore, it is important to give our partners a no-strings-attached attitude. If we cannot, then we need to choose otherwise.

I suppose I also have to own up. I'm no different from Treasure, because I was also caught, like everyone else, in endlessly repeating, self-destructive behaviors. Treasure's case has reminded me that we must throw away the old and welcome the new, healthier concepts that can expand beyond familiarity of the misleading concepts that we learned from our families, schools, and society. They need to be discarded and replaced with healthier ones.

My responsibility now is to help Treasure identify her lifelong distorted beliefs and romantic myths, so as to eliminate them and to enable her to grow and develop into an *emotionally mature adult*. Self-responsible spouses recognize that wanting to change their spouses never is a realistic option, and that to get busy changing themselves is.

Meinecke also mentions in her book the following important key ideas from relationship experts.

- It is better to be unhappy alone than unhappy with someone.

- Romantic love is not the only joy in life.

- Personal happiness does not depend upon being coupled.

- The golden key is to look within and assume responsibility for one's own life's choices and happiness.

LIGHT AFTER DARKNESS (THE FINAL DECISION)

Shanghai, China

It is almost eleven months down the road of treachery; the Shanghai winter seems colder for Treasure this year. Her favorite outfit of washed out jeans and soft cashmere top hugs her body comfortably tight and shows off her sportive figure. Although she's in her fifties, Treasure has always been mistaken for ten years her junior. Yes, in recent months, she's lost some weight, which she cannot afford with an already slim body. From afar it looks as if the big lounge chair has swallowed her up. With her hair tied back loosely in a ponytail, Treasure appeared more relaxed through the web-camera.

"Treasure, for a long time doing nothing was the easiest and least threatening way to handle your relationship with Xavier. You were assuming that the situation between you and Xavier would not get worse. Or at least you hoped so. You hoped that if you did nothing, things would at least stay the same, if not improve. You can say it's your wishful thinking. Who knows? Probably Xavier was thinking the same way, only acting out differently."

"The status quo in a relationship cannot be maintained indefinitely. The situation will change even if we do nothing, because ultimately we are not in control of all the variables that can affect our relationships. Besides, nothing is meant to stay the same forever.

"Ask yourself these questions. What do you think would happen to your marriage if a) Xavier continued to put his needs first; b) he couldn't find a job he likes the next time he lost his job; c) your practice in Shanghai takes off and you wish to stay put instead of moving to his next work destination; d) you insist on your boundaries; e) there was another tragic death in the family; or f) you get really sick?

"Any of the above events can create a shift in the balance of your relationship. From my professional experience, I know that when an event disturbs the precarious equilibrium of a dysfunctional partnership, the contaminator's abusive behavior toward his or her partner automatically escalates."

"You wouldn't even know what hit you. So, Treasure, you might get by with accepting things the way they are, but doing nothing in the long run is a dangerous game."

The fervent hope of every woman I've treated in a narcissistic relationship is that somehow something will happen that will make it all better. Each woman wants to believe that one day her partner will come to his senses, take her in his arms, and say, "Darling, I know I've been a jerk and terribly insensitive to your needs. Forgive me. I'll never hurt you again. I love you, and from now on things will be the way you wanted." As a matter of fact, Xavier already expressed similar words to you and yet took no concrete actions to support his verbal promises. Treasure, do you see that now?"

"Yes, Alicia, I know my relationship with Xavier is far more likely to get worse than to get better, particularly when he stopped therapy. People become more entrenched in their behaviors as they get older; they are less willing to change. Particularly when he always carried the saying "People don't change" on his lips. I know he was really trying to say "I don't want to change". If I accept the situation the way it was, I am renouncing my right to be treated with the respect and dignity to which I am entitled and was ignored for all these years. Alicia, I've come to realize that I've enabled Xavier to disrespect my needs and feelings. You could say that I've arrived at a place to make that final decision ---Alicia, I've decided I'll be moving out in two weeks."

"Do you mean you've decided to leave Xavier for good?" I asked.

"Yes, Alicia, I think so. I feel so scared, and I really dread him. I don't know who he is anymore, and the more I look, the less I like what I see."

As I hung up the receiver, I couldn't help but think: *I've always known Treasure will find her way. It is I that am still lost and afraid to face my own shadows. How I can help my clients and yet find it so difficult to walk the walk myself?* I decided it was time to call Mitch, my therapist.

LEARN TO LOVE THYSELF

Brisbane, Australia

Unhealthy Dependency Love

I have been using psychiatrist Eric Berne's model of Transactional Analysis to help clients understand their personality development and communication pattern. What I did not know is that his model has proven especially effective in understanding dependency love in relationships, or what Mitch would call addictive relationships.

"Mitch, are you saying both my client and I are addicted to love?" I cried out to my therapist.

"No, Alicia, I'm not saying that at all; what I'm saying is that you might have signs of a potential love addict, so be careful."

Soon after the session with Mitch, I reflected on my own distorted beliefs and possible signs of love addictive behaviors. I cannot help but think maybe I've not managed to help Treasure to explore hers. I could see certain similar characteristics in her. Like me, she's been over-adapting to what others want; she has boundary issues, fear of letting go, fear of the unknown; she gives love excessively to get love (the disease to please); she attempts to change her husband, demands and expects unconditional love, looks outside of herself for affirmations and worth, and fears abandonment.

According to Eric Berne, everyone consists of three ego states: the parent, adult, and child. If healthy, the parent ego state nurtures and protects. The adult ego state analyzes, thinks, and solves problems. The child ego state feels and identifies needs. The child ego state is where the myths lie, and addictive love begins when needs are not met. "It's not safe to get close," "I'm not lovable," "I'm not good enough," "Love hurts," "Men can't be trusted," and "Women are manipulators"—the list of myths goes on.

The adult ego state is supposed to gather information that can help solve problems rationally, not emotionally. Unfortunately, the information stored can be inaccurate; for instance, if a role model as we are developing demonstrates that the solution to deal with human tragedies and uncomfortable feelings is to lie, deny, ignore, numb or have a drink, that "how-to" is recorded in our brains.

Parent ego state, as its name implies, is meant to provide unconditional love, protection from harm, and a soft place to fall; it also serves as a teacher. We learn to set healthy boundaries and learn ways to lead healthy, productive lives. Unfortunately, this state can also be critical, controlling, rescuing, interfering, manipulative, and enabling and denies the inner child with statements like: "You're a bad boy!" "Nice girls don't get angry!" "Big boys don't cry," "If you don't stop crying, I'll give you something to cry about," "I'm busy, don't bother me!" "Nobody will like you if you act like that," and "Be Daddy's good girl, and do as I say."

According to Berne, only the natural child (NC) ego state is present at birth, and at this state it totally relies on the external world and caretakers around to satisfy its needs.

At six months, the little professor (L.P., the adult in grownups) appears and realizes that the natural child needs food, warmth, and protection, physical and intellectual stimulation to grow and develop. It is vital to find ways to continue having caretakers around to satisfy its needs, or the child dies.

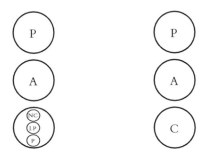

Then, at about the age of three, the third part of the child ego state, the parent (P) in the child, develops. This stage, which lasts until age six or seven; the parent (P) in the child or also known as the *Adapted Child* is the trained child who develops social awareness but sometimes feels very not-OK.

We are born with no sense of what's right or wrong. Our first sense of conscience develops very slowly from interacting with our environment, especially with our caretakers. In most cases would be our parents who are our primary teachers or role models. It is the Parent-in-the- child: *Adapted Child*, with the aid of the Adult-in-the-child: *Little Professor,* we learn to avoid pain and get approval. We learn to adapt to the "Shoulds", "Musts", and "Oughts" of our parents and other authority figures … we adapt to the dysfunction of our family through the use of survival skills.

As children continue to develop to the age of 7-11, that is the "magic age" of Santa Claus, fairy tales, and monsters. Hence, when parents say, "You make me so mad sometimes!" or "You make me happy!" children take them literally, believing they have the power to control their parents' feelings and they (the parents) controlled theirs. Children tend to think in black and white—no gray—because at that age that is the only way a child's mind can work.

Understandably, such dynamics are normal in a child; however, in an adult they can be problematic if the adult continues to have beliefs that turn love into unhealthy dependency.

As I was reviewing Treasure's file, Treasure herself came to the realization that more often than not, when her mother was distressed about Treasure's grievances with her sister, Liz, she would tell Treasure, "Oh, Liz is all stressed out from her studies. You're a good girl; let it go." Treasure would listen to her mother's wishes and let things slide.

Treasure's story may sound rather poignant and sweet: a child caring about and obeying her mother's wishes is considered one having the most valued of virtues in Asian culture—filial piety. But Treasure as a child needed her mother to be an adult who would care for her and protect her. Like most children of that age, she was not yet able to analyze what really was happening. Instead, Treasure believed she might lose her mother's love if she insisted on her own needs being met.

As a child, Treasure needed justice, truthful information, and reassurance, and she didn't receive that. She needed her Mom to say, "From what you just told me, it seems Liz is all stressed out from her studies. Come with Mommy, and we shall listen to her side of the story. If I find Liz treated you badly, she owes you an apology." Instead of receiving maternal comfort for her hurt child ego state, Treasure was invited to take care of both her sister's and her mother's anxious child ego state, by suppressing her own hurt and needs in the process.

Unbeknownst to Treasure's mother, she had taught Treasure to care for both her sister and herself at Treasure's own emotional expense. Treasure clearly continued to do so in her adult relationships, particularly the one with Xavier. From an immature child's point of view, Treasure's decision was creatively adaptive: *I'll stop feeling angry, hurt, and needy and take care of Mother's wishes.* And it did seem to work all those years that Treasure imagined her mother as her protector. Mom did stick around—until she killed herself, and Treasure's world came tumbling down. That's when years of anger and resentment set in.

No wonder Treasure continued her unconscious pattern of shutting down her feelings and needs; she unconsciously chose needy men who supported her distorted beliefs as a child. Thus, she actually got what she wanted in her codependent relationship with Xavier. He was psychologically self-serving and prevented Treasure from having her needs fulfilled. As a matter of fact, Xavier supported the conclusions she learned as a child: *My needs are not important. I have the power to make others happy if I fulfill their needs, and in return they'll love me.* The tragedy is that Treasure needed and had a right to her own feelings, desires, and support; she needed to be cared for without always having to put other people's needs first.

In addictive love the ties of dependency run from one partner's inner child to the other. Addictive lovers believe that they need to be attached to someone in order to survive and that the other has the magical power to make them whole. That's what Meinecke mentions in her book the three common misconceptions of love: 1) It's better to be unhappy with someone than to be alone; 2) as lifelong partners, we are supposed to fulfill each other's wants and needs; and 3) love cures loneliness.

This is why addictive love is dysfunctional. Addictive lovers believe they can be whole only when someone completes them. In the popular movie *Jerry Maguire*, Tom Cruise expresses his love for Renee Zellweger with "You complete me." This is definitely not healthy. The pervasive feeling that something is missing attracts them to unconsciously seek out others to meet their unmet needs. Unfortunately, they are often out of touch with their real needs and therefore seek out people similar to the original person (a parent) who did not have the capacity or knowledge to meet those needs in the first place. In other words, in order for Treasure to heal, she needed to face her fears and tell the truth by drawing boundaries and *putting her needs first*. She needed to start loving *herself*.

Back Stage

SELF-REFLECT AND AWARENESS:

1) What are some of the love myths you learned in the past that you suspect is causing you unhealthy behaviors in your relationships?

2) What are some of the reasons why you are hoping the status quo in your relationships can be maintained indefinitely?

3) What are some of the reasons why you are not practicing self-care and self-love in order to cultivate healthy relationships?

FINAL CURTAIN

Growing Old is Mandatory and Growing Up is a Choice

Beauty fades but stupidity stays with you forever.

Judge Judy

Scene 12

GROW OLD OR GROW WISE

Shanghai, China

I know this is going to be our final session. Treasure has her hair down, and she has gained some weight since we last Skyped. It warms me to see twinkles in her eyes, and for an instant, I know she's going to find her authentic self and becomes whom she truly desires.

"Alicia, can you hear me?"

"Oh, I'm sorry, Treasure. What was that?"

"I was asking for a summary—my final curtain if you will."

"Do you wish me to sum up our work here for the past nine months?"

"Yes, please. I'm still a bit puzzled by what you mean by childhood traumas. I still think I had a pretty good childhood."

Barbara Kiao, L.C.C.

"Ah, that. Okay. When I say childhood traumas, I include traumas that you are not aware of, such …"

"Do you mean my illusion of having Dad and Liz as my adversaries, the way I portrayed my mother as my protector, and her chronic depression?" Treasure interrupted.

"Yes, Treasure, exactly. We tend to reenact our childhood traumas or hurts in our adult relationships. For instance, you unknowingly married a man who cannot love back. You were demoralized and furious when you first found out his betrayal; you blamed many of your relationship issues on him. Since Xavier was the one who broke the trust, I called him the contaminator in the relationship; your self-righteous anger was justified. He had to change so that you could get rid of those negative thoughts in your head. When he chose to terminate therapy, you interpreted his actions as a statement about you. You felt unimportant, unattractive, and rejected."

"While these feeling-related thoughts could be explained given Xavier's addiction and maladaptive behaviors, you couldn't stop them even if you wanted to. It runs deep. His feelings of shame, fear, and inadequacies are a bottomless pit. If he does not seek professional help, his behavior will stay an endless vicious cycle that has nothing to do with you. When you came to me, we looked at what was going inside you that kept getting triggered in the relationship. I believe we managed to get clarity for you?"

"Yes, indeed. I suppose I could put an end to my own story, eh?" Treasure tossed her hair back and continued. "I now realize my past experience was the filter through which I was judging myself and Xavier. As I told you before, I really thought I had a good childhood. As we explored, I remembered all those times of being ignored and feeling lonely. I remembered being verbally abused by Liz and my parents. When I asked them for help, they blew me off. I decided that all the negative things they said were probably true, because my father always sided with Liz; and even my Mom, my only protector, deserted me."

"The feelings I had were exactly what I felt when I learned about Xavier's betrayal and maladaptive behaviors. Every time he failed to answer my questions and was being disengaged, in my mind I heard him saying, *Treasure, you are stupid and your opinion is not important to me.* I would take it a notch higher and hear, *you're not lovable and I'm going to leave you for someone more attractive and loving.* I had been working hard to change Xavier to become the partner I needed him to be—someone to affirm what my family had failed to affirm. I realized I had to heal my childhood trauma, and I had to believe in my importance, beauty, and intelligence—I mean, deep down to my core existence and not believing superficially. How am I doing so far?" Treasure asked with a smile and raised eyebrows.

"Very good; I'm impressed," I exclaimed.

"You know what, Alicia? I also would like to share with you the one thing that I was ashamed to admit for a while … I've mistaken real independence for some kind of fake independence based on the safety net of my marriage."

"Treasure, that takes courage and I appreciate you sharing that with me."

"Thank you so much, Alicia. Want to hear how I imagined Xavier understands his therapy if he would have chosen to do the work?" Treasure asked casually.

"Sure, if you wish," I replied.

"Okay. Here we go. I think this is what Xavier would say: 'I was in denial all along and refused to think I had a problem until I realized that although I had an attractive, loving wife whom I loved, I could not stop my compulsive use of pornography, internet affairs, extramarital relationships, and alcohol dependency. I was absolutely overwhelmed by my personality assessments with my therapist. I'm glad Treasure finally caught me, after a decade of lying and deceit. It was absolutely exhausting."

"'I'm slowly realizing we both brought stuff to the table from our pasts, and I took most of hers personally. I still have no idea why I'm so afraid of my past childhood;

my therapist said I'm like a welded submarine, that I simply won't allow anyone in. I had a hard time feeling anything, but I thought this was a "man thing." I didn't realize I had been suppressing my emotions for years, decades; I'm fearful of the beast inside me."

"'I can't remember much of my childhood; I have much to explore and learn, and it's possible that I blocked parts out. I believed I was bad and not worth loving. I was hoping Treasure would magically rescue me from my distorted beliefs, but that was futile. I'm working hard to find out what truly happened to me when I was young that led me to such self-destructive behaviors. I don't doubt we had legitimate love in our relationship; I know I love Treasure, but there has always been a hidden need to fix our wounds. To top it all, I never learned to assume responsibility for my actions. I had distanced myself from Treasure by having meaningless sex with other women and mistreated Treasure, so when she found me out it was she who chose to end the marriage, and not I, a destructive pattern resulted in feeling that I am controlled by external events; instead, all along it was my own choices that caused me to suffer. As long as I continue to deny my own destructive ways, real change is unlikely, because my attention will be focused on changing my environment rather than myself. Of course, I did not know this until I started therapy work. I'm slowly learning to open up to Treasure. My goal is to be able to recognize my triggers and be able to talk about them with her. Our couples' counselor said we'll learn to appreciate the little boy and little girl in each of us, and that we could exchange our stories in the future.'

"What do you think, Alicia? Pretty good, huh? I guess this is as objective as I could get and sort of a fantasy, another made-up story ..." Treasure looked straight at me with a broad smile.

"Yes, I'm impressed that with your creativity you managed to walk in Xavier's shoes. How does that feel?" I asked.

"Mm, I feel lighter and less angry. Besides, I like happy endings," Treasure replied.

"You will get your happy ending, just not the way you expected it to be."

"Yeah, Alicia, I am sure you are right. I also wanted to thank you for your kind assistance. You've helped me explore the side of me I never knew existed and showed me the way to recovery. I now know that I have to forgive myself for everything. You've been most supportive when I was vulnerable and most patient when I resisted change. I can't thank you enough." Treasure gave me her usual invigorating smile.

I could see love and certainty in her eyes. I knew for sure then that she would finally live her authentic life instead of living Xavier's.

"You're most welcome, Treasure. I also wish to thank you for sharing your story with me, and most of all for your courage, strength, and honesty. I do realize how hard it is for people like us to admit and share our vulnerability. People think just because we have knowledge of psychology that we are exempted from life's lessons; and because we can help them, we can also help ourselves at all times. God knows we all have blind spots and shadows." We looked at each other and laughed simultaneously. I shall miss our sessions, and I will miss Treasure. I know my own work has already begun.

Scene 13

FORGIVE THE
UNFORGIVABLE

Brisbane, Queensland, Australia

Shakespeare's Hamlet asked, "To be or not to be?" I would say a more appropriate question is "How to be?" to forgive or not to forgive?

Xavier always avoided all conflicts, even healthy debates. He used his first marriage to Michellene, as his shield: "I don't wish to argue with you. I hate arguments; that's why I got divorced." I'd say he felt inadequate most of the time, believing he was never good enough. But now I know, he had his secrets. When his occasional affairs didn't help, he would pay women to do whatever he wanted; he just wanted their attention, maybe because he wasn't scared with them, and it was easier for him to perform sexually because they were strangers who didn't need anything from him. His father was a POW in Russia during the Second World War; that did not help. He lived in a household that internalized family shame-based beliefs and most likely trained him to seek approval of others, an approval he could not give himself. It is exactly this that caused him to become dependent on the praise and positive attention of others to feel good about who he was. He had a sensational need to seek *outer esteem*, which is esteem through others.

He never learned to internalize self-worth and value, so he was in a perpetual state of looking for affirmation and validation. Having a verbally abusive father, the message he got was that no matter what he did, he wasn't good enough. His mom was like a ghost: emotionally and mentally nonexistent. Like Treasure, he was an impressionable kid who, like most kids, just wanted to be loved. He had a hole so big and deep in his gut, only alcohol and sex would fill it up temporarily.

As for Treasure, her household operated with a theme: "Don't talk. Don't talk about any problems or feelings you might have. Do what you're told. And most important, never talk outside of home." They didn't air their dirty laundry, whatever it was. They were to show only good feelings, which of course meant to suppress anything that weren't a happy face. Don't feel. Treasure was highly disciplined and obedient. She took that discipline into her adult life and became a party girl and love dependent. And whom would she choose to be her partner? Not a rage-alcoholic, not a workaholic, but another type of addict.

Meinecke so eloquently writes in her book, "Regardless of age and stage, anyone can choose to practice self-responsibility, gain emotional growth and reap the benefits of mature and everlasting love." Amen!

So, what's that got to do with forgiveness? I daresay in all unhealthy relationships, all parties need to accept responsibility for the ways they may have contributed to the perpetuating harmful dynamics and their own pains and sufferings, and then learn to forgive them and go on.

I find most people get confused by the concepts of forgiveness and reconciliation. They are two separate things. Forgiveness is something we can do all by ourselves, something we can choose to make happen. Reconciliation, however, is a two-way street.

How important it is for Treasure to forgive Xavier, her parents, Liz, and, more importantly, herself? I'd say it's absolutely vital, for her own well-being. Oftentimes, people misunderstand the meaning of *forgiveness*. They think that when one forgives, one's sending a message to the offender that what she or he did is okay. On the contrary, to *forgive* is to cancel all debt and release the shackles that one is wearing around one's ankles and that are weighing one down. More eloquently explained, carrying a grudge, refusing to forgive, is like feeding yourself poison and hoping the people who wronged you would die! Treasure needs to forgive them and, more importantly, to forgive herself. To own up to the wrongs on her side of the street makes true forgiveness possible.

Forgiveness needs compassion and empathy, and compassion comes from our own experience of injury. I have faith that Treasure has compassion for herself, and in turn can learn compassion for Xavier's maladaptive behaviors, learn that his choices had nothing to do with her. They were not personal, although it felt personal.

I remember I once saw in a documentary film about the Re-unity, Reconciliation Camp in Rwanda: A facilitator explained that forgiveness is not a suppression of anger. Forgiveness is asking for a miracle, the ability to see through someone's mistakes. The ability to see the truth that lies within all of our hearts, he also says that forgiveness is not always easy; at times it's more painful than the wounds they suffered, and that it could be more painful than the wound that was inflicted upon them. Nevertheless, the first step to forgiveness is the *willingness to forgive*. Ah, such words of wisdom, and if the Tutsis can forgive what the Hutus did during the Rwandan genocide in 1994, I'm sure Treasure can see through Xavier's mistakes, and to the truth that lies within her heart.

Phan Thi Kim Phuc. *Who?* You may ask. She is the girl in the world-famous photograph of a naked nine-year-old running toward a camera, her clothes shed because they were set alight with napalm that had been dropped on her village by the US Army during the Vietnam War. I read in a magazine that she expressed to the reporter that she believes that they (Vietnamese and Americans) have to move on to help each other, and that she wanted to *forgive* the people who caused her suffering. She said she did and so she is free from hatred and bitterness.

I could continue to name a whole list of people who have had and are still practicing forgiveness, but the few world-famous characters who pop into my mind are the "Iron Orchid," Aung San Suu Kyi of Burma; the late Nelson Mandela; and the Tibetan spiritual leader, the Dalai Lama.

As I was writing Treasure's story, Lindy Chamberlain's news was the headline in all major newspapers and TV stations once again. It's taken Lindy thirty-two long years to clear her name after being accused and jailed for the killing of her baby daughter, Azaria. A different coroner in Australia has ruled that a dingo stole baby Azaria from their campsite back in 1980. I've not read Lindy's autobiography, but I'm most certain she's endured immense pain and treachery to finally put to rest the past. It was the fourth inquest, on June 12, 2012, that accepted that Azaria was indeed taken and killed by a dingo, and the cause of her death was changed on the baby's death certificate. Reporters are asking if all those who had spread rumors and thought and accused her of wrongdoing will finally stop and maybe even apologize to her. Fat chance; I can't help but think it's so hard to contemplate the additional challenge associated with letting go of resentment when the people who harmed you don't look like they'll be apologizing anytime soon. Maybe it's even more tormenting when we just don't understand why they did what they did. It definitely takes an amazingly strong and kindhearted human to let go of a need for explanations and to forgive anyway. I'm only guessing, for I'm far from being this evolved myself, but I have more faith in Treasure.

Scene 14

LOVE AND RESPECT: ACCEPT AND APPROVE OF THYSELF

Brisbane, Australia

↑   ↓

Shanghai, China

In recent years, science shows that one has better physical and mental health, better relationships, and better spiritual well-being when one forgives. I suppose to love and respect self; it is only wise to not be burdened by the negative energy that hate and vengefulness brings.

Knowing when to call it quits is loving self; and loving self is to have compassion toward self.

Success lies in being able to retreat at the right moment and in the right manner. The success

> is made possible by the fact that the retreat
> is not the forced flight of a weak person but
> the voluntary withdrawal of a strong one.
> The *I Ching*, or *The Book of Changes*

My clients ask me frequently whether addictive relationships can be saved. This is indeed a good question, and the answer I give is that some relationships can be saved, and others can't and shouldn't.

> When you keep wishing and hoping
> he will change.
> Robin Norwood

Oftentimes, relationships become addictive and dysfunctional when obsession and unhealthy dependency are present. If a love addict stops obsessing and being too emotionally dependent on his or her partner, sometimes the relationship can be salvaged. Unfortunately, more often than not, a love addict tends to select an unhealthy partner who also has an addiction of his or her own, and unless this partner also focuses on self-recovery, the relationship will not survive. Therefore, the goal is each partner's own growth and development, and it is that personal growth that contributes to the growth of a healthy relationship. Having said that, it is no walk in the park, because it requires a lot of patience, and at the same time, there is a fine line between being patient and loving too much. Not all recovering love addicts can walk this fine line.

As I was contemplating my own predicament, it suddenly dawned on me that for me to start loving myself, I need to follow Treasure's model for my husband, who much like Xavier radiates a tough mystique that grows out of a basically selfish, withholding, and guarded nature.

I was drawn to what I thought of as strength in his insensitive toughness, his machismo, and secretly felt potentially safe and reassured by that "strength." Who am I kidding? I say "potentially," because I never quite feel part of his "strength," since he rarely shares or opens up to me. Like Treasure, I also did all the emotional work for the two of us; he would set the stage, and I, "loving too much," would of course dance around, always attempting to read his mind. Mind you, I was very good at it too. I can see now that he never allowed me to get too close. I loved it and hated it at the same time. I know I'm drawn by the very characteristic I am bound to and so wanting to change.

Sure, I knew he's too emotionally guarded for my taste, but I thought this would all change once he realized he could trust me. I'm not going to hurt him the way his first wife did. She didn't love him enough. I thought I am special, what Caroline Myss would identify as the "being special" archetype. That I understood his secret tendencies, I saw them as reflecting his self-control, acting as a shield of his past hurts. I thought I was "special" and that I could make him want to change. Oh, how many times he was insensitive to my needs, and what did I do?

Like Treasure, I talked myself into believing his insensitivity was because I hadn't communicated my feelings to him clearly, and so the disconnect must be my fault. For years, I didn't know why I was so unhappy. I kept convincing myself that if I loved him enough, he would open himself to me. And when he did, I could finally reap the treasure that surely lay within. Now I know it's my own fantasy, my endless hoping he'll change and be the person I so wanted him to be—it will never happen.

Xavier's tough, controlled outer shell concealed a tougher, more controlled inner core. Xavier claimed he loved Treasure, but she seldom felt it, and he never showed the demonstrative affection she wanted and needed. Treasure interpreted his guarded, withholding nature as mystique. What she found was that instead of standing guard over some hidden treasure, he in fact was desperately trying to protect his insecurity from exposure. When she realized this on that spring day of 2009, Xavier's strength was transformed in her eyes to brittle, crumbling defenses. His once wonderful mystique turned to fear.

The welded submarine either fears his dependency needs or has managed to convince him that he doesn't have any. He is very attractive to many women who mistake this trait for strength and self-containment. But the problems soon emerge as the woman begins to want more. We all experience love, at least in part, through feeling needed by our partner, needed emotionally. The "submarine" can't allow himself to need anyone enough to form an intimate, satisfying bond. To do so would require him to confront his fears of weakness and vulnerability. Decades of scarred hurts may have destroyed his capacity to feel that deeply.

A loving relationship is to have my partner dependent on me, not blood-suckingly so, but needing me emotionally and vice versa; this is interdependence. Unfortunately, "welded submarines" are like clams; they will never allow themselves to be dependent enough to be able to form close, sharing relationships. No matter how warm Treasure's love is, it will never melt Xavier's protective shield (definitely not without genuine self-reflection and examination).

I daresay what has been misguided in the pursuit of Xavier is the failure to correctly identify his real strengths and weaknesses. Treasure may have believed she possessed the magic potion (her love) to change him, to allow him to feel safe to love, but she didn't. The fact of the matter is, the more Treasure loved and cared for him, the further she was driving him away. Intimacy is his enemy because it scares the hell out of him. That's why he betrayed

Treasure's trust, and it is only wise and loving for Treasure to face her fear of letting go. And let go she did.

I suppose some can say Treasure lost at love, but as I looked into her eyes, I saw differently. She's very much alive and kicking. However, it never ceases to amaze me how heartless and unconscious some people can be, especially people who are close to us, who are supposed to love us and yet act so shabbily. Not only are they oblivious to their behavior, but even when they realize, they have no desire to repent or to change for the better.

We know the reasons for their reluctance to change. Maybe through our compassionate eyes, we see no absolute fault or evil and learn to forgive them and also ourselves because we also know their pain, for we all have been there before.

Now that it's nearly done, I feel good to be facing the final curtain, and realizing the reason I did all that is that Treasure's story is also part of my life's journey and meant to be my closure. I hope this book will also touch your heart and that you'll share the knowledge with others that, regardless of age and stage, it is never too late to choose to practice self-love, self-compassion, and self-reflection, to face fears head-on so as to gain emotional growth and reap the benefits of emotional maturity and divine love.

As I slowly look up at the reflection in the mirror, our eyes lock, and we both let out our invigorating smiles.

Back Stage

SELF-REFLECT AND AWARENESS:

1) Are you someone that cannot move forward due to unforgiveness?

2) If you know there are no limitations, would you wish to choose *fear* over love?

EPILOGUE

Where There Is Fear, There Is No Love.
Where There Is Love, There Is No Fear.

Unknown

I want to know: Did the title of this book fool you?

I am definitely not encouraging divorce, nor am I against it. What I wish to say is that we do not need to judge it. When we judge those who took this path, we shame them, and where there is shame, there is fear. Where there is fear, there is no love. There would only be vicious cycles of maladaptive behaviors being passed down from generation to generation.

After more than a decade in helping couples to gain further intimacy in their relationships, I daresay we tend to take the easy way out too often too soon. We are fearful that we will not find happiness again if we do not change our external situation, and so we tell ourselves by changing partners our problems will be gone and all will be well again. On the flip side, we are so fearful of what others would say or think of us; or worse, we are so fearful we may lose all the hard-earned wealth that we tell ourselves we sacrifice our happiness for the children's sake. So we stay in unloving relationships, not realizing that by doing so we are modeling unhealthy relationships to our children.

Of course, relationships need work. Having said that, there are indeed some relationships that cannot and should not be salvaged; nevertheless, we must leave no stone unturned before we take the path of divorce, particularly when there are children involved. Until we choose to take the road less traveled of self-reflection, self-love, self-compassion, and self-forgiveness, we will continue to blame others for our own mistakes.

It is only when we consciously practice self-love that we can give and receive fearless love because where there is love, there is no fear, and where there is fear, there is no love—only obligation.

The good news is that we all have the power to choose—love or fear. I don't know about you, but I have learned to choose love. I wish the same for you, only without the painful lessons.

BIBLIOGRAPHY

Berne, E. *Games People Play: The Basic Handbook of Transactional Analysis.* New York: Ballantine Books, 1964.

Brown, B. *Daring Greatly,* Gotham Books, a member of Penguin Group (U.S.A.) Inc., 2012.

Carter-Scott, C. *If Love Is a Game, These Are the Rules.* Milsons Point, NSW, Australia: Transworld, 1999.

Meinecke, C. *Everybody Marries the Wrong Person.* Far Hills, NJ, USA: New Horizon, 2010.

Stoop, D. *Forgiving Our Parents, Forgiving Ourselves.* Ventura, CA, USA: Regal Books, Gospel Light, 1991.

ABOUT THE AUTHOR

Australian licensed clinical counselor Barbara Kiao, has been providing counseling and life coaching to individuals, couples, and organizations for more than a decade.

She was born in Hong Kong, spent her most impressionable years in Canada, and has been an Australian national for twenty-four years. She conducts workshops, seminars and lectures worldwide and currently resides in Shanghai, China, where she has her own private practice.

www.barbarakiao.com
contact@barbarakiao.com